Designing-Women's Lives

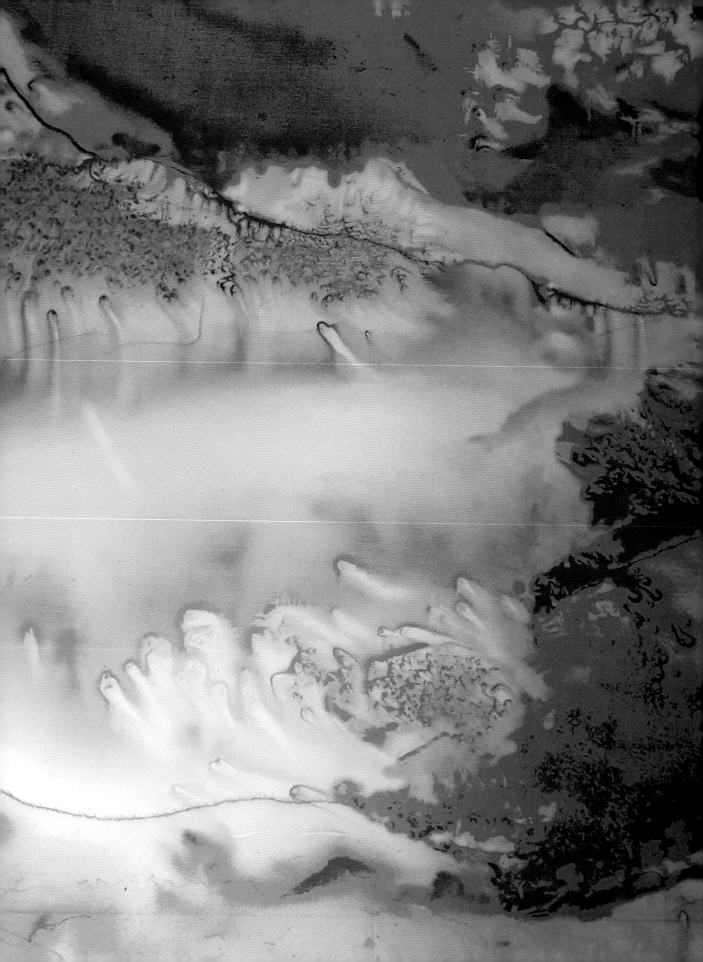

For my mother and father

ORO Editions
Publishers of Architecture, Art, and Design
Gordon Goff: Publisher

www.oroeditions.com
info@oroeditions.com

Published by ORO Editions.

Author: Toby Israel
Book Design: Pablo Mandel, Silvina Synaj / CircularStudio
Project Manager: Jake Anderson

10 9 8 7 6 5 4 3 2 1 First Edition

ISBN: 978-1-954081-11-6

Color Separations and Printing: ORO Group Inc.
Printed in China

ORO Editions makes a continuous effort to minimize the overall carbon footprint of its publications. As part of this goal, ORO, in association with Global ReLeaf, arranges to plant trees to replace those used in the manufacturing of the paper produced for its books. Global ReLeaf is an international campaign run by American Forests, one of the world's oldest nonprofit conservation organizations. Global ReLeaf is American Forests' education and action program that helps individuals, organizations, agencies, and corporations improve the local and global environment by planting and caring for trees.

Designing-Women's Lives

Transforming Place and Self

Toby Israel

Table of Contents

Acknowledgments

When I first floated the idea of this book, a dear colleague advised me that I might be stepping on landmines by dealing with gender and place-making issues in this age of political correctness. I thank all those who helped me navigate through this project's sometimes-tricky terrain. I'm so grateful to all who believed in this book and helped me bring it safely home.

First and foremost, I so appreciate that Denise Scott Brown, RIBA, Int. FRIBA, Hon. FAIA; Margo Grant Walsh; and Esther Sternberg, MD, all agreed to be interviewed for the book. I continue to be so inspired by their "heroine's stories." It takes a willingness to be vulnerable to share your lived experience with others who might benefit from such telling. For this, I also thank Angela O'Byrne, FAIA, for providing her "Women on Fire" speech for these pages.

It was a pleasure to work with Olga Strużyna, Sarah Seung-MacFarland, Ph.D., Suzan Ahmed, Ph.D., and "Katya", as students and contributor-colleagues whose "self-place" tales I've followed with such interest. The curiosity and enthusiasm they expressed helped me stay the course regarding this book and the relevance of Design Psychology for the next generation.

Similarly, it was such fun to work with Jennifer Morgan and Binnie Thom on their home projects. I appreciate that they gave me permission to profile their lives and house transformations here. Their input, including both practical and moral support during all phases of this endeavor, was invaluable.

Equally remarkable and so appreciated was the time and energy contributed by the manuscript's outside readers. I will be forever grateful for the brilliant insights and editing of Amy Beth, Ph.D., MLS, Digital Resource and Scholarship Librarian at Guttman Community College, The City University of New York. She played a crucial role in steering this project in the right direction and helping me thoroughly weave its theoretical thread. Similarly, I thank Deanne Nicholas, NCIDQ, AIA, NCARB, LEED GA, associate professor at Drexel University, Westphal College, director of MS Design Research, MDes. She graciously provided her thoughtful and knowledgeable interior design educator's perspective. With good reason, I trusted architect Richard S. Rosen, AIA, principal at Perkins Eastman, to contribute his ever-insightful comments for which I am so appreciative. As usual, Marian Hamilton was a pillar. Her regular feedback on each section of the manuscript helped me pinpoint where I needed to make cuts for this book to be accessible to women who aren't professional place-makers.

Similarly, Laurie Cohen, Ph.D., professor of Organization Studies at Loughborough University, provided not only feedback at the early stages of the project—she remained a trusty advisor on practical and academic issues throughout. Michael Roy Layne, Ph.D., ASLA; Renne Rocklin, LCSW; and Elizabeth Young, LICSW, all played similar roles and were so willing to provide feedback on the book's early development.

I've decided that my new favorite people are librarians. I could not have completed this project without them. Special thanks go to all of the librarians who assisted me at the Princeton Public Library and to Gabriella Karl-Johnson, Architecture Librarian, School of Architecture, Princeton University, as well as the other librarians there, who were so helpful.

I am equally indebted to those who dug into archives to help me obtain photographs for this book. I especially thank Emma Brown, research assistant at VSBA, Inc., for her patience and fortitude. Likewise, I thank Laura Sovetti, Reference and Instruction Specialist, Special Collections and Archives, Robert E. Kennedy Library, Cal Poly, San Luis Obispo; and Jennifer Lightbody of The Glasgow School of Art. Special thanks also to Amanda Nagai and to Robert Funk.

I very much appreciate the speedy replies, advice, and great expertise of Jake Anderson, ORO's managing editor, who smoothly guided this book as it moved along. Thanks go to graphic designer Raghu Consbruck. As this project progressed, she patiently worked with me to deliver the book's graphic material in top form. Sophie Loring's editorial work likewise was so valuable and appreciated. I thank my brother, Jayadvaita Swami, editor, publisher, and teacher for his gracious, valuable editorial and practical input throughout. I remember Gloria Shapiro for her eagle-eye proofreading and for so much more.

I wrote large portions of this book not only on my back porch, but while spending time in the transcendent places of retreat that sponsored my residency. For this, I want to wholeheartedly thank the Atlantic Center for the Arts, especially Jim Frost and Executive Director Nancy Lowden Norman. The Seaside Institute's Academic Village likewise afforded me warmth and comradery as I wrote. The Wiawaka Center for Women in Lake George, NY, was my idyllic home away from home for many summers. I thank Artscape Gibraltar Point on Toronto Isle for allowing me to write while surrounded by real-life sailboats and the energy of artists. Then, too, because I was able to go into the woods at Lacawac Sanctuary in Lake Ariel, PA, I had solitude and a beautiful, comfortable setting in which to write.

I also thank the Princeton Y.W.C.A. Breast Cancer Resource Center for their help and support during my illness, for championing the *Robe to Wellness* project, and for hosting my *Oasis by Design Psychology* lecture/workshop. For this, I wish to thank Kara Stephenson and am especially grateful to Laura Martin, who I will remember as a unique and special soul. Naomi Drew M.A. also deserves thanks for sparking my interest in women and place when she arranged my talk to the women of Princeton's Pot Lucky Society. I also offer thanks to Micene Fontaine, executive director of Design Arts Seminars, Inc., for helping me spread the word about Design Psychology. Thank you to the American Institute of Architects for providing me with access to its Women's Leadership Summits.

Last, but never least, I want to thank and honor my dear friends on both side of the Atlantic including, especially, Debbie D'Arpa, Jere Tannenbaum, Ken Kowalski, as well as those others mentioned above (you know who you are). It is because you fed and watered me, cheered me on, and remain such an important part of my life that I was able to finish this book.

Introduction

This will be a conversation just between the two of us about how design of depth and connection between self and place can be a form of personal transformation. In 2003, with a similar goal in mind, in my book, *Some Place Like Home*,[1] I introduced Design Psychology, "the practice of architecture, planning, and interior design in which psychology is the principal design tool." Back then, rather than answering questions like, "Would my blue chairs look good against my yellow walls?" I wanted readers to ask the deeper question, "How can I use my past, present, and future story of place and self to create emotionally fulfilling environments?"

Interestingly, I've noticed that it is mostly women who've approached me to learn about Design Psychology. Why mostly women? I thought maybe it was because the field was something new: Design Psychology's digging through the *emotional* bedrock of one's life/environment is so different from the objectively oriented, traditionally male-dominated field of architecture that's *master*-minded our built world.

Over the years, I've watched women struggle to fit into that world. Given their struggle, I thought about the landmark book, *Women's Ways of Knowing: The Development of Self, Voice, and Mind*.[2] I wondered, "Is there a 'women's way of knowing' crucial to place-making that's been discounted?" My speculation about women and Design Psychology led me to ask a bigger question, "Is there, in fact, a whole realm of human experience that needs to be laced back into the built world?" If so, rather than struggle to fit in, shouldn't women, especially, be pioneering a new way of making environments?

My questions about women and Design Psychology nagged at me, since I suspected that answers to them might have wider implications for creating place. I turned to writing this book as my quest to find answers and gain insight about designing-women, the psychology of design, and myself.

As you'll see in **Part I** here, I first dug deeply into feminist design literature to understand the challenges facing designing-women. I define "designing-women" in this book, as "women who make *place*" including, especially, female architects and interior designers. My literature review gave me an overview of the challenges faced by female place-makers. Still, I wanted to dig down further to examine the lived experience, the personal stories, of key designing-women pioneers. Was there something about their journeys or their sensibilities that led them so successfully to ride (and sometimes make) feminist waves?

With a historical overview in mind, I began to examine the life/work of architect Julia Morgan (1872–1957), now recognized for the amazing 700+ buildings she designed. Yet, since lived experience inevitably is a perspective told first-hand, I then reached out to interior architect Margo Grant Walsh, whose illustrious career at the Gensler design firm began in 1973. She broke the glass ceiling when she became managing principal there. Similarly, my search for insight led me to the door of architect/planner/icon Denise Scott Brown who won the American Institute of Architects' Gold Medal in 2016 at the end of her amazing career. You'll read here how these women not only helped transform their professions—they navigated their own personal transformations.

In fact, since my training is in environmental psychology, a field that studies how people affect environments and environments affect people, I examined their stories through that psychological lens. To do so, I took Grant Walsh and Scott Brown through the same Design Psychology series of exercises I'd previously used with famous design world men.[3] As a result of excavating the "environmental autobiography," the personal history of place of both of these females, I unearthed the fuller tale of how Grant Walsh triumphed over the oppression of the Chippewa reservation of her childhood and Scott Brown navigated through anti-Semitism in her South African homeland. Most relevant to my research was that I learned how their lived experience could be "read" in the design of their public projects and in their private homes.

As I became more and more engrossed in examining ways women know, design, and struggle in the world, I then went on the road to conferences to listen to more tales. Paying attention to our female stories seemed particularly vital since, when it comes to affecting real change, as author Elena Ferrante points out, "Power Is a Story Told by Women":

> There is one form of power that has fascinated me ever since I was a girl, even though it has been widely colonized by men: the power of storytelling. ...Storytelling...gives us the power to bring order to the chaos of the real under our own sign, and in this, it isn't very far from political power... The female story, told with increasing skill, increasingly widespread and unapologetic, is what must now assume power.[4]

When I sat back from this road I traveled, I understood that designing-women often have repressed their *culturally* nurtured "women's way of knowing" (their feeling sensibility, for example) in order to achieve "success": Females so often struggle to assume their professional as well as personal power.

Thus, in **Part II**, I suggest how, rather than struggle to fit in, women can break new ground by tapping into their lived experience to find their liberated, even transcendent voice. To show you what I mean, I write about how, despite her rootless childhood, even famous feminist activist Gloria Steinem created her home as a catalyst helping her achieve a healthier sense of self. Then, too, I tell of creating my

Women can break new ground by tapping into their lived experience to find their liberated, even transcendent voice.

Design Psychology's exploring, recognizing, and articulating of primal, authentic experience of places reframes any architecture, interior design, or even planning project at hand and gives it a higher purpose —to create environments that connect us to our human selves.

own healing "oasis by design" while undergoing treatment for early-stage breast cancer. Esther Sternberg, MD, a scientist and healing places author, also talks here about ways she consciously and unconsciously created "healing home."

I hope that by telling all of these stories, I'll show you how messages about self and place remain buried deep inside your psyche. Since they unconsciously rise to the surface anyway when we design, I hope I'll get you thinking about how such messages and memories consciously can be mined. You can use the best of your lived experiences to transform places, practice, and even yourself. Such deep "design from within" constitutes a radical new way of creating environments.

To illustrate what I mean, **Part III**, "Applying Design Psychology," includes case studies of women with whom I and others worked to use Design Psychology's exercises to harness their inner power via psychologically powerful place. Some of the women discussed are professional designers, some are psychologists, and others were just clients seeking to make a change during some significant life-stage. The Design Psychology process they went through addressed their challenges of growing into adulthood, of partnering, of grieving, or of standing strong alone. I hope these examples of their use of color, shape, texture, space layout, and special objects inspire you to use the psychology of design on your way forward. I provide you with access to the online Design Psychology's exercises to do just that.

Overall, I want to encourage a mind-shift in architecture and interior design practice and education. This book is a rallying cry for designers and design schools to include the psychological/social considerations, not just the aesthetic/functional aspects of place-making, in their work and curriculum. Design Psychology's exploring, recognizing, and articulating of primal, authentic experience of places reframes any architecture, interior design, or even planning project at hand and gives it a higher purpose—to create environments that connect us to our human selves. Mental health practitioners long have recognized ways that creative art therapy techniques using the visual arts, music, drama, the written word, and even dance can help ease life crises or act as catalysts for personal growth. Similarly, the case studies I've incorporated here illustrate how Design Psychology not only can be embedded in the traditional design process, but also in therapeutic practice. Hopefully, in the future, therapists will explore this new use of place-making to pioneer new healing paths.

Regardless of whether you are a professional place-maker, a psychologist, or just an interested reader, since I want this book to be both a professional and personal conversation about how design can transform, I've used my women's "lived experience" writer's voice here: Within each main chapter, I interweave sections linking 1) my own journey to change/grow, 2) women and place-making literature, and 3) stories of the designing-women I interviewed, met, or admired. Then, too, this book is for readers of any gender identity since all of us face life-crises, challenges, and passages—since we are all on our journey to become our full self. Hopefully in reading the book you'll notice your own patterns—your own journeys. You'll have your own "aha!" moments. You'll perceive more clearly how you and others can create transcendent, liberating places that enable each of us to find our voice and design soul.

PART I:

Designing-Women's Lives

CHAPTER 1:
Designing-Women's Worlds

Draperies, My Mother, and Me

Over the years, like a rapt archeologist, I've unearthed the past-place stories of famous design-world *men*. I've delicately examined each detail of their childhood homes and hangouts until I saw the full picture of how these fragments fit together to form the foundation of their famed male-made designs. Now that I've stepped back from my digging, I feel guilty as I realize I haven't actually examined the environmental stories of women.

Curious about female place-makers whose stories I may have left unheard, I began to read the literature about feminism and design while on my back porch. Ah! But then a blue jay in a nearby tree began sweetly chirping on and on. Its song lulled me into musing about my mother, born in 1923. Mother became an interior decorator. She really wanted to be an actress before she married and had children. That creative fire was doused by her stern, hard-working immigrant mother, the family breadwinner, who heard "actress," and thought "fallen woman." Still, women with passionate hearts like my mother need to find avenues of expression.

So, my mother struggled to find a path for herself. She became the first family member to go to college. She went on to teach and do set design at Douglass College. By her mid-twenties, my mother left behind teaching and set designing, married, and gave birth to my older brother and to me. In her early homemaker years, she made all of my little lace dresses, directed the school plays, and helped my father at his paint and wallpaper store. But it wasn't enough. She felt stifled and so she parlayed the advice she had been giving at the family store into a decorating business run out of our home.

Most female homemakers of that generation weren't expected to work except within the home where the dictum was: MAKE WARM HEARTH = HAPPY HOME. Most men were out doing the "real work." For my beloved father, the man-burden of real work at "the store" meant he had two heart attacks and died by the time he was fifty-four, when I was only sixteen.

My mother continued to work, and from an early age I can remember tagging along with her from designer showroom to showroom as she chose fabrics and furniture that transformed her clients' lackluster homes. Via these outings I learned to carry any color in my head, to arrange furniture in a space, imagining people within it, and soon I could spot a beautiful, jaunty lamp or a cushion with a tale to tell.

At first the world of interior decorating provided a creative outlet for my mother and many other marginalized homemakers to both express and transform their psychic and home interiors. As time progressed, however, the idea that "just any-one"[1] could decorate a home became denigrated and was seen as trivial by those wanting interior "designers" to be viewed as professionals like architects or lawyers. In this new wave, designers were *in* and decorators were *out*.

Such a push to put interior design on equal footing with male-dominated design professions seemed a step in the right direction in an era where women rightfully were demanding equal rights. Yet the push to professionalize also had a boomerang effect of re-marginalizing some women for whom home was the only canvas on which they could paint their most colorful selves. My mother, for example, began to feel she was a fraud despite her creative talent and professional success since she did not possess any "real" interior design credentials.

What were the real credentials? Look closely and you'll realize that even those women who became the standard-bearers of the profession, like former debutante Dorothy "Sister" Parish, had no formal design training. Interestingly, Parish wrote about how her interior design philosophy was influenced by childhood experience of place:

> As a child, I discovered the happy feelings that familiar things can bring—an old apple tree, a favorite garden, the smell of a fresh-clipped hedge, simply knowing that when you round the corner, nothing will be changed, nothing will be gone. I try to instill the lucky part of my life in each house that I do. Some think a decorator should change a house. I try to give permanence to a house, to bring out the experiences, the memories, the feelings that make it a home.[2]

Yet Parish was no psychologist of design. Hers was nostalgia decorating where "chintzes, overstuffed armchairs, and brocade sofas with such unexpected items as patchwork quilts, four-poster beds, knitted throws, and rag rugs led to her being credited with ushering in what became known as American country style during the 1960s."[3]

Right there laid a schism because these messages, like waves, went back and forth: *Housewives should create the ideal home! Look to the high styles of the past! Search for your own unique expression!* Meanwhile women entering place design professions were hearing, *"Just find a way to join the exclusive, male place-maker's club!"*

Digging deeper now to understand, I realize that such mixed messages sent mixed signals to my mother and to women in general about what it meant to be a successful homemaker, designer, or just a fulfilled woman in the world. It was confusing. Now I am wondering what messages you and I got from our homemakers about how to create a home oasis, places, or a life.

I remember the living room of my childhood, split-level home. My mother transformed that unremarkable room into what I now think of as a dramatic French provincial stage set. It had a Louis XV-type couch covered in gold brocade fabric. That front room's bay window was covered in heavy gold draperies. Cut-glass crystal dishes were arranged carefully on a marble coffee table. We rarely sat on that couch, used those dishes, or saw light come through the window. The room just told the story of the high-style "good taste" at the time.

The real story behind the scenes took place in our family den; also a carefully decorated but more informal space, its comfortable, mid-century modern couches were bold in a '50s-style peacock blue and gold abstract print fabric. In the years before I reached my teens, my father and I would grab the couch's bolsters and together we'd lie on the soft-carpet floor to snuggle and watch T.V.

All that changed when he had his heart attack and began to fade away. I'd still lie by his side but then, surreptitiously, I'd watch to see if his chest was moving up and down—watch to see if he still was breathing—if he was still alive. My mother and his doctors knew that he was dying, but no one told me or him. That's the way it was at the time. There were secrets behind our front door, behind those heavy draperies.

Every day, every hour, I lived in the dark with that axe of death that hung over us. I knew intuitively (as did my father) what fate lay at our doorstep. Yet the message was, "maintain the beautiful veneer." I tried to part the draperies to reveal the truth, yet confusion—not just about window dressing or couches or even what it meant to be a woman—but about life and death swirled in my head as I struggled to figure out exactly what was going on.

Now, it's still painful for me to think back to this first chapter of my environmental story and the disjoint between the beautiful outer display and the turmoil inside. Still, it's important to reflect, as I now realize that this drama probably set the stage for me to found Design Psychology. It is perhaps because of our family troubles that I became passionate about helping others examine their environmental stories. Rather than imbibe mixed messages or feel they have to hide, I wanted to help free up other women, especially, to create authentic places that enhance and express the true essence of their lives.

Herstory of Place-making

I returned to reading further to learn about women in interior design and architecture and feminist waves, but I kept drifting back to the stories of the females in my family. Their ways of making spaces helped me understand my mother's taste and how women have made "self"-in-place throughout the generations.

Take my Great Grandma Rosa, for example, a highly educated city girl who got married off to a poor Hungarian farmer in the mid-1880s. I'm sure Rosa was shocked to leave behind the cityscape of Hungary's grand Neo-classical and

Romantic buildings, only to end up in a three-room home with mud floors, white-washed walls, her thirteen children, and husband for whom she had to cook. Like so many females in her era and before, she had no choice.

Yet as a rare villager who could read and write, Rosa could "escape" by practicing her true art—*storytelling* during quilting bees. The tales Rosa told to her eager sewing circle of stitching women transported them from humble kitchens to far-off places of adventure and romance. Most of all, Great Grandma and her circle dreamed of escaping poverty and pogroms.

That's why at the turn of the century, one by one, each of Rosa's offspring, along with a wave of European immigrants, came to America to find a better life. My Grandmother Stella arrived first in 1914, alone at fifteen. She worked, lived humbly, married, had children, and eventually opened a small corner store near New York City's docks, where she charmed sailors into buying dry goods.

Once successful, Stella created the beautiful home she never had in Hungary. Hers was an eclectic style of blue velvet curtains, a dark wood Gothic Revival dining room, oriental carpets, and cloisonné vases. Such eclecticism, "thrived in America… perhaps because there was so little past on which to build."[1] All this set Stella's scene. It was the design of an interior that told the story of one woman's upward mobility in the New World.

While Grandma was never really rich, others made it big in America at the turn of the century. Many expressed their self-worth via their wealth. In particular, "The idea of importing something from the past that would bring with it culture, style, and status became an obsession that offered to the newly rich and powerful in America some identification with the European aristocracy."[2]

To meet such needs, up to the late 1800s, male architects and tradesmen were the professionals creating interiors.[3] At the turn of the century, too, men (not women) dominated the emerging American interior design profession.[4] Elsie de Wolfe, an actress who later became known for her stylish taste, changed that trajectory.

In fact, de Wolfe, born in 1865, often is credited with inventing the field and term "interior decoration." She was hired by members of her social elite made rich by the Industrial Revolution.[5] Her clients wanted lavish home interiors that expressed their power and prestige, not their primal connection to place. De Wolfe tapped into their desires. As such, her decor positioned the new field of interior decoration as a profession for the upper crust.

In doing so, de Wolfe rejected what came before her: William Morris's anti-elite approach, popular back in the Old World, which lauded authentic, handcrafted decoration inspired by the British countryside (or Great Grandma Rosa's village?). Morris's rustic Arts and Crafts style emphasized nature and simplicity as an antidote to the ever-increasing depersonalization resulting from the mass production of the Industrial Revolution.[6]

De Wolfe hated Morris's style. Alternatively, she preferred what's been called a more "feminine" aesthetic of brighter colors, lighter and softer fabrics[7] including flowery printed chintzes. She combined such elements to create rooms that exuded eighteenth-century French or English high-style.[8]

The Morris Room. Victoria and Albert Museum, London.
Victoria and Albert Museum, London.

By rejecting a simpler craftsman style, was actress-reborn-as-decorator de Wolfe actually championing "interior décor as a stage set" rather than as authentic space? De Wolfe certainly sparked a taste shift. More importantly she spearheaded a gender shift as interior decoration became one of the few acceptable professions for women—especially women of taste during her era.

Overall, De Wolfe's success was all the more possible because of the *First Wave* of feminism that appeared in the late nineteenth and early twentieth century. During this wave, women were fighting for basic legal rights such as, astonishingly, the right of married women not to be owned by their husbands. Likewise during this time, women were seeking the right to vote, own property, and enter into contracts.[9] Given Great Grandma Rosa's plight, such strides couldn't come too soon.

At the onset of the twentieth century, women wanting to become architects were marginalized, too. Even design schools that supposedly welcomed women in the early days of the twentieth century remained patriarchal. The famed Bauhaus, established in 1919, for example, combined art, architecture, craft and industrial design in an attempt to abolish all hierarchies in the arts.[10] Although it claimed to offer women absolute equality, the school's founding director, Walter Gropius, worried "that the number of females studying there would damage its credibility."[11] Thus, behind the scenes, he put a quota on applications by females, increasingly directing them to less "challenging" subjects.[12]

Throughout most of the twentieth century, then, it's no wonder that the architecture profession remained overwhelmingly male.[13] By the 1930s, however, further splintering occurred even within the interior professions. The very term interior *decoration* morphed into the term interior *design*. Why the name shift? The idea that anyone could design a living space often was seen as trivial perhaps because of its "association with the domestic"[14] with mere "women's work."

Some scholars believe the newer term interior design, and later the term interior architecture were adopted to legitimize these professions and align them with the "more serious" (think: more *male*) business of architecture.[15] Especially given this gender imbalance in architecture/interior design professions, some suggest that such separate labeling represents an "othering" that continues to denigrate and marginalize interior designing-women.[16]

Perhaps such herding of women into separate professional pens seemed appropriate in de Wolfe's time when "women were considered to have a 'natural bent for interior decoration.'"[17] Even when it came to practicing architecture, in 1902, the editor of "The British Architect," summed up the attitude of his day when he deemed women "temperamentally unfitted" to create good architectural design considering:

their "lightness of touch," "changeability," and "charming" decorativeness lacking the masculine "strength of handling," "steadfastness of view," and "judicious reserve" needed for architecture. He maintained that "in the supreme and essential qualities of fine architecture a woman is by nature heavily handicapped."[18]

With such faulty assumptions pervasive, many educators also taught that women lacked objectivity and the ability to make critical judgment as well as to think independently. When asked why there were no women's dorms on campus, in the early 1900s, one university president replied, for instance, "Women in large groups tend to become hysterical."[19]

Importantly, such statements are a symptom of a deeper problem beyond the historical/cultural/political gender challenges I've discussed here. Such faulty generalizations about the essential psychological nature of women have limited opportunities for females in the world of place-making and beyond.

In this regard, let me pause now to say that by even discussing female versus male place-makers, one runs the risk of assuming that gender-identity is binary. De Wolfe, herself, lived with another woman throughout her marriage. Moreover, early on, gay bachelors in Europe:

> *used interior design as a means to express their personal identity and character. In fact, they often used their personal home design as a means to counter what were viewed as the rigid constraints of domestic interiors of their time. ...Their personal design aesthetics gave them an outlet for creativity that could occur within the safe confines of their personal homes.[20]*

Thus, these gay designing-men may have come closest to using place-making as a means of authentic self-expression, albeit behind closed doors. In later years, many gay men entered the interior design profession, yet stereotypes about what it meant to be gay, male, or female persisted. Were there and are there still actual differences between the "male" and "female" psyche when it comes to designing environments? For years theorists have posited that men were better than women when it came to spatial relationships, that women don't do science, and that they're not good at reading maps—the reverse being true for men.[21] Such assumptions may have deterred many women from even thinking about studying architecture or engineering.

The *Second Wave* of feminism that blossomed in America in the 1960s–1980s helped explode such myths. Besides raising issues around equality and discrimination, this wave challenged women to examine sexism inherent in their personal lives.[22] Betty Friedan's landmark book, *The Feminine Mystique*,[23] published in 1963,

The Elsie de Wolfe Residence, Villa Trianon Versailles, France.
Painting attributed to William Bruce Ellis Rankin (1881-1901). Wikipedia Commons.

Faulty generalizations about the essential psychological nature of women have limited opportunities for females in the world of place-making and beyond.

challenged the idea that women were fulfilled by just being stay-at-home wives and mothers. Friedan put her finger on "the problem that has no name,"[24] women's dissatisfaction with what she saw as such domestic imprisonment. Friedan inspired a wave of women (including my mother) to step out of their domestic roles and become competent, working professionals.

Thankfully today, myths about women's abilities continue to be decisively challenged. In her book, *The Gendered Brain*, Gina Rippon, professor of Cognitive Neuro-imaging, uses the latest research to explain *How New Neuroscience Explodes the Myth of the Female Brain*.[25] She critiques an "essentialist" belief that the brain possesses a gendered biological essence that is "fixed and innate."[26] In her research she's found very little difference between male and female brains.

While such myth-busting helps create strides, *cultural conditioning* still exists. Quintessential myths still told about women may encourage females to develop or at least display stereotypical female versus male personality traits. When it comes to gender and emotion, for example, in his book, *Emotional Intelligence*,[27] Daniel Goleman points out that, "Parents, in general, discuss emotions—with the exception of anger—more with their daughters than their sons. Girls are exposed to more information about emotions than are boys,"[28] who aren't encouraged to express their feelings. Thus, many males become "largely unconscious of their emotional states both in themselves and in others."[29]

Goleman goes on to note that when girls play together, they do so in small groups with an emphasis on cooperation, while boys play in larger groups, with an emphasis on competition. Goleman further refers to the hundreds of studies that suggest that, on average, women are more empathetic than men.[30] Nevertheless, theories claiming "that the female brain is predominantly hard-wired for empathy, and that the male brain is predominantly hard-wired for understanding and building systems" have been debunked.[31] In *Better Boys, Better Men*,[32] the author Andrew Reiner points instead to cultural conditioning since boys often are taught to "man up."[33] As a result, Reiner concludes, "Much of the disconnect for boys in their relationships with friends and family boils down to a reduction of their identity, which often leads to emotional isolation. This begs the question: How can boys be authentic when we rob them of the language of their emotions?"[34]

Cultural conditioning has an impact. In her article, "A Feminist Approach to Architecture,"[35] environmental psychologist Karen Franck explores that impact by examining women's own experiences in architecture and in everyday life.[36] Franck reviews literature by feminist authors who posit that women and men learn and come to "know" differently, based on their early experiences. She surmises that many view our underlying relationship to the world as one of *connection* for women versus *separation* for men.[37] Franck furthermore cites feminist thinkers who see the masculine design world as proffering a dualistic perspective wherein qualities of "connectedness"—emotion and subjectivity, especially, are viewed as separate from reason.[38]

I began to play with the words (below) that Franck, the writers she discusses, and other feminist theorists use to describe the culturally conditioned sensibilities of female versus male designers:[39]

Women = *Emotion, subjectivity, connection, ethic of care, cooperation, home and family life, and labor of hand, head, and heart*

Men = *Objectivity, separation, ethic of justice, public life, competition, and hierarchical dualisms*

Hmm. I know men who show emotion, have an ethic of care, and relish home and family. I know women who seem disconnected and competitive. Franck, herself, cautions that differences between men and women, "is suggestive at best."[40] Still, I sense that such gender conditioning might be one reason why more women than men gravitate to Design Psychology. It's a field that by nature deals not only with what you *feel* in places, but ways your whole sense of self and place are *connected*—intertwined.

Overall, reflecting on my family's self-place stories helped make real and relevant the feminist theories I was sifting through. Besides knowing about my female ancestors, I wanted to know more about the real-world experience of other female place-makers who struggled to establish their professional and personal identities. Did such struggles have implications for the psychology of design?

When considering the significance of stories, of our narratives, some feminist art and architecture critics think we should dismiss the biographies of individuals completely since "biography reinforces the myth of bourgeois individualism and deliberately obscures the structural inequalities of Western society that maintain a hierarchy based on gender, class, and race."[41] I totally disagree and side with author/therapist Clarissa Pinkola Estes who (using construction as a metaphor) links storytelling+place-making+emotions:

> *Stories set the inner life into motion, and this is particularly important where the inner life is frightened, wedged, or cornered. Story greases the hoists and pulleys, it causes adrenaline to surge, shows us the way out, down, or up, and for our trouble, cuts for us fine wide doors in previously blank walls, opening that lead to the dreamland, that lead to love and learning, that lead us back to our own real lives as knowing wildish women.*[42]

Curiosity made my own adrenaline surge as I began to learn about the life of one designing-woman, whose tale of making it in a man's world I'll tell you next.

Julia Morgan, FAIA

Embarking on my autobiographical dig into the lives of female place-makers, I began by reading about Julia Morgan, the first female to receive the American Institute of Architecture's Gold Medal given to "individuals whose work has had a lasting influence on the theory and practice of architecture."[1] Historically, the award's mostly all-male winners have received this honor in their lifetimes. Regrettably, Morgan's medal (conferred in 2013) came fifty-six years after her death.

I'd visited California's San Simeon, the extravagant Mediterranean-style castle she'd designed for magnate William Randolph Hearst. Years later, by chance, I came across Asilomar, a rustic Y.W.C.A. retreat complex she created based on Arts and Crafts-style influences. Seen in juxtaposition, these projects are so different from one another, it's hard to believe they were conceived by the same architect. In fact, Morgan was a prolific architect who mastered many styles. Did her vastly different styles reflect different chapters of her personal story? As a Design Psychologist, I wanted to know if her work reflects her "inner" evolution, not just her professional versatility. I delved into her environmental autobiography to find out.

Born to a well-to-do family in 1872 and raised in the San Francisco Bay area, Morgan's parents encouraged her to pursue her education. Accordingly, she was the third woman ever to graduate from the University of California, Berkeley, with a B.S. in civil engineering and the first woman admitted to the famed École des Beaux-Arts in Paris where she completed her diploma certificate in architecture.

Although she opened the door for women, once Morgan stepped inside the École, she found herself in a male culture of separation rather than connection. The École immersed her in the all-male, wildly competitive, academic, "object-oriented," "style,"- and "star"-conscious education that was to become prototype for architecture schools developed throughout the United States and the Western World.[2] There she was rigorously trained in an ornate form of neoclassical design like that of the Paris Opera House.[3] No doubt her "steel-trap mind and will of iron"[4] helped her navigate this daunting education. Arguably, however, the École also furthered a personal/professional disconnect in Julia Morgan by sending her the implicit message: mute your feminine identity. Rather than make waves, Morgan chose to take on the persona of a non-controversial, accommodating architect:

Morgan conscientiously down-played gender and cringed at efforts to identify her as a "woman architect." She presented herself as an asexual professional. Dressed in

Julia Morgan.
Julia Morgan Papers, Special Collections and Archives, California Polytechnic State University.

simple, unassuming suits she projected a neutral image. ...To overcome the emotionalism associated with women, Morgan displayed an even temperament at all times... [Morgan] was quiet and subdued, and yet she was quite firm in getting her ideas over. She demonstrated commitment by becoming a workaholic, devoting almost every waking hour to architecture while subsisting on a few hours of sleep and a diet of chocolate bars and coffee.[5]

Casa Grande, San Simeon, designed by Julia Morgan. Shutterstock.

Given the cultural context of her time, Morgan felt compelled to hide her emotions just as cultural conditioning still pressures men into hiding their feelings today. Morgan not only faced the pressure to assimilate into architecture's male world, she had to deal with oppressive practice. After graduation she returned to a job in California, where her boss bragged that he had a wonderful woman designer working for him "to whom I have to pay almost nothing." Hearing this, Morgan quit and opened her own practice.[6] She remained determined, fearless, intelligent, and practical, but didn't consider herself a feminist despite the rise of the first-wave women's rights movement during this period.

Morgan built up her firm and designed buildings at a time when women were taught to focus on growth, human relationships, and beauty. While continuing to project a gender-neutral outer image, Morgan did meld that image with the caregiver qualities associated with women in her day. Although she never married or had children, she displayed an ethic of care by treating her staff as an extended family—financing the education of some employees, sharing profits, and giving gifts to workers' children.[7]

Then, too, she opted to work "with the tide" to create projects that she described as "sincere and good"—projects associated with the feminine-assigned role of nurturing or service.[8] Thus, for instance, she designed residential or institutional projects like numerous Y.W.C.A.s.

Interestingly, for example, in creating "cozy" parlors and libraries for Pasadena's Y.W.C.A., Morgan exhibited sensitivity to the connection between design and human emotion/relationships.[9] Similarly, in the dining hall of San Francisco's Y.W.C.A., she specified small, separate tables rather than long institutional rows to prompt familiarity. Closely examining the social needs of residents, she displayed a sense of empathy in terms of other design decisions for that facility:

Hearst Social Hall, Asilomar, designed by Julia Morgan. Courtesy of Aramark.

In contrast to comparable male residential facilities such as Y.M.C.A.s, those for women were very restrictive. To compensate, Morgan provided diverse amenities.

At the facility in San Francisco known as The Residence (1929) she gave occupants private dining rooms and kitchenettes on the upper floors. When the Y.W.C.A. board objected noting, these are minimum wage girls, Morgan answered, That's exactly why they need pleasant surroundings and opportunities to entertain friends.[10]

In fact, when designing the buildings at Asilomar and in other projects, too, Morgan worked to create such a humanistic, people-centered "feeling" quality—an essential "personality," an "animation" in each of her structures.[11] By emphasizing feeling and a person-centered aesthetic was Morgan an early psychologist of design? Moreover, did her buildings express *her* authentic self?

Looking for clues about the impact of her environmental autobiography, I studied a photo of her childhood home, a Victorian-style dwelling that was dark, cluttered, full of bric-a-brac, and heavy curtains! Few if any of the seven hundred+ structures Morgan created suggest that she recreated her childhood environment in any work of architecture. That is, except in one case: the San Francisco buildings she, herself, bought in the 1920s and lived in until her death in 1957. Originally two adjoining Victorian houses, she converted them into one dwelling with several apartments including one for herself. Glancing at a photo of that adult home, the curved bay windows and the triangular capitals that adorn its door and window appear reminiscent of her childhood residence in Oakland.

Yet then I noticed something strange. On the left side of her adult home, the whole second floor has been removed—eliminated! Reportedly Morgan did this to let light into her own unit. Still, it's as if something's been chopped off. The lack of balance is all the more strange given that Morgan's other buildings, regardless of style, seem so well-proportioned.

Julia Morgan's *childhood home*, Oakland, California.
Julia Morgan Papers, Special Collections and Archives, California Polytechnic State University.

As a Design Psychologist, I've learned by now that the houses we create tell our stories of self. On the one hand, Julia Morgan harked back to her childhood roots in her choice of her adult Victorian home. Yet once ensconced there, in dedicating herself so completely to her career, did she stymie her personal evolution? Had she stifled—cut herself off from her emotional needs as unconsciously symbolized in her home's truncated second story?

Then, too, when it came to other architecture projects like ones influenced by the American Arts and Craft wave, Morgan created architecture that (like her) was understated and blended in with the natural environment.[12] Yet while so many of Morgan's projects were wholesome rather than "monumental,"[13] conversely, others boasted ornamental styles of the past, like the Spanish Renaissance style San Simeon displayed. No doubt, the elaborate expression at San Simeon reflected Hearst's own hedonism[14] rather than Julia Morgan's personality or penchant. Apropos of this, she was considered "The Client's Architect"[15] always striving to meet her clients' needs, not her own:

> *The key to Julia Morgan's success as an architect, and one of the qualities that set her apart from many of her male contemporaries, was that she conducted her practice with a completely client-oriented philosophy. Julia saw her role as the head of a team that included her staff and her clients. She would listen carefully to the ideas, wishes, and goals of her clients, getting to know them and their needs before beginning a design project for them.[16]*

In fact, Julia Morgan "carefully crafted [an] image as a non-controversial, accommodating professional."[17] Similarly, she wasn't a big ego architect. Despite her success,

Julia Morgan's *adult home* **(right), San Francisco, California.**
Photograph by Amanda Nagai.

she avoided publicity while the male architects of her day courted publicity for their object-oriented and style-conscious work.[18]

Women traditionally have been encouraged to be accommodating and self-effacing. On the one hand, these are laudatory qualities and Morgan's approach suggests an empathetic, collaborative sensibility and approach to architecture. On the other hand, however, she may have paid a price for embracing such a persona and for focusing on doing "sincere and good"[19] work since her "low-profile and gender contributed to her professional invisibility."[20] Yet, as professor emeritus Diane Favro suggests, referring to "sincere and good" work, "if these aspects of architecture are thought unimportant, then perhaps the priorities of the architecture profession, not the gender of the architect, should be evaluated."[21]

Merrill Hall, Asilomar, designed by Julia Morgan.
Courtesy of Aramark.

In the end, the scope and quality of Julia Morgan's work *was* monumental. Her stamp was one of excellence achieved through a variety of styles and mastery of light, space, and scale.[22] Her range of styles reflects her prodigious talent and sensitivity. Still, throughout her career, Morgan understandably felt compelled to mute her female identity to survive as an architect given the constraints of her day. In doing so, she may not only have ceded her professional visibility, but her personal inner life. Increasingly a recluse, she died at age eighty-five. Thus, overall, Julia Morgan's story remains both a totally inspiring yet cautionary tale that illustrates the peril of assimilating into a group rather than fully claiming one's own personal/professional identity. In her time, perhaps Morgan could do little else. Thankfully, in our time, she's increasingly celebrated as an iconic, trailblazing architect.

Thankfully, in our time, Julia Morgan is increasingly celebrated as an iconic, trailblazing architect.

Roman Pool, San Simeon, designed by Julia Morgan.
Shutterstock.

CHAPTER 2:
The Heroines's Journey

A Woman's Search for Meaning

Back on my screened-in porch, musing about Julia Morgan, I notice that bold blue jay plunk itself down again on my pond's edge. It's pecking, staring – at its reflection? at a worm? at me now? Its feathered head is cocked. Is it asking me an existential question or maybe asking me for a confession?

Perhaps I'm just projecting because, in truth, like Julia Morgan, I've often felt the need to repress my emotions. In my case, maybe I did so because of my family's secret-keeping around my father's illness. I learned early on to hide my feelings. Still, I didn't really want to mute my feeling self or become the hardest working person in the graveyard like my dad who wondered at the end, "What was life about?" After he died, I searched for ways to open up and struggled to make meaning in my life.

I tried to reclaim the magic of being alive through art—by writing or drawing. Perhaps the ghost of my grandpa, an artistic spirit, had whispered in my ear, "Life, however short, has meaning." Goodness knows I needed to transcend since I was drifting in a deep, dark fog after my dad's death.

One day I grabbed a charcoal pencil and began to sketch. At first I wasn't sure what to draw. I let my emotions guide my soon-deliberate strokes. As the hours went by I forgot about the dark cloud over me and instead yanked open each door inside myself to find out where my hiding heart crouched. By the time I was finished drawing, I'd sketched a woman full of life emerging from a cocoon. In doing so, I'd drawn and thus had visualized my woman's rise. At that moment, stepping back to view my charcoal image, I profoundly understood the transcendent power of the arts to deeply touch the soul.

Soon I went off to university. I'll tell you how my life and career progressed from there. Still, be aware that timelines only tell a factual tale. The deeper narrative that drives our lives often remains unconscious. Did Julia Morgan, for example, *consciously* decide to hide part of her identity (like a chameleon) to survive? My guess is that she just lapsed into camouflaging to move through male territory. Perhaps, no matter what the era, we are all part chameleon, making choices in order to thrive.

As a Baby Boomer, I had more choices than Julia Morgan or the other women in my family. The burgeoning "second wave" Women's Liberation Movement of the 1960s provided me and other females with more options. I thought about becoming a psychologist to help others find direction but how could I do that when, in truth, I still was floundering? I considered becoming a lawyer. It would be a practical profession and ensure financial security. (My immigrant ancestors would be proud.) I enjoyed logical analysis yet my ability to gnaw the bone of an argument to death wasn't a quality I wanted to feed. Then, too, intellectual argument remained unbecoming for a female at that time.

Despite the widening array of options for women, teacher, nurse, secretary, or wife-volunteer remained the typical, culturally encouraged career choices in the early 1970s. Predictably then, perhaps, lock-step after graduation, I went with the tide and became an English teacher to do "sincere and good" work, but also to try to make meaning for myself and for my students.

I did my best to electrify my 8th graders with the transcendent power of poetry, hoping to use the magic of words to draw kids out of *their* cocoons. In my annual review though, my principal simply complimented me on my bulletin boards. He imparted his "wisdom" to me: "A school is like a factory. Just as a factory needs to be sure all of the pieces fit together, so children must receive all of their educational parts." I imagined affixing a tiny bulletin board to his forehead. I pinned a note on it saying, "Good-by factory."

I needed a new job. Intuition (or my artistic grandpa's ghost) pointed me further toward the arts. Rather than crank out my principal's middle school mannequins, I took a job in an experimental public elementary school's "Project Unicorn"[1] teaching the basic skills through the visual arts, music, dance, and...*architecture*.

Although female architects still were rare at the time, Betsy, our "Architect-In-Residence,"[2] worked with me and my 6–10-year-old students to build a tire playground for our school. Today I "dig" carefully into people's environmental psyches. Back then, these children dug with abandon into real dirt to build the playground they helped design. The opposite of factory workers, they shoveled past pebbles, marveled at worms, and planted big, black rubber tires.

What did you do as a child
That created timelessness
That made you forget time?[3]

In my own "aha!" moment, I realized then that such primal, childhood, playful "work" in the environment gives us the gift of our most blissful, emotional sense of place: "That fluid, early experience of surroundings flows as fresh perception as the child experiences everything as new, transcendent."[4] "[They are] poised...halfway between inner and outer worlds. ...in love with the universe."[5] As adults, more often than not, this magical place-self bond lies below our level of consciousness—dormant within us. Why not uncover it?

Inspired by this question and by our architect-in-residence, I considered becoming an architect. Throughout my childhood I'd watched my mother transform clients' homes. Perhaps it was inevitable that I would do the same. Yet her interior decorator's career took place in the '50s when creating a post-war, upbeat "Pleasantville" was in vogue. I was *questioning* my world of home-as-make-believe and, as a child of the '60s revolution, questioning the American Dream.

I flipped through architecture school catalogues, but most programs focused on the function, history, or aesthetics of place-making with no mention of the psychological impact of our environments. I perused what seemed like 1,000,000,000,000,000 photos of *buildings* in architecture magazines, but none featured *people* inside their rooms! I wanted to create spaces that integrated, not cut people off from *human* experience. (Or perhaps I was seeking to restore my own human balance?)

Uncertain which path to take, one day I went to a lecture by Dr. Maxine Wolfe, a pioneering environmental psychologist. I'd never heard of environmental psychology. At Princeton University in a room filled with men in black suits and ties, Wolfe (dressed in blue jeans) spoke about how a "High Art" psychiatric facility designed by star-architect Richard Meier drove patients crazy with its reflecting glass and maze-like hallways. She explained how environmental psychology, a field championing environments for people, provided an antidote to such myopic design. Here, at last, was human-centered design profession. It was as if a bolt of lightning hit me!

Shortly thereafter, I applied to The Graduate Center of The City University of New York's Environmental Psychology Program. Once admitted, I was gripped by courses on Children's Environments and on Environmental Meaning that described *emotional* attachment to place. As part of my studies there I read the landmark article "The House as Symbol of Self"[6] by landscape designer/thought-leader Professor Clare Cooper Marcus. It was as if another door opened.

Referring to Jungian psychology, Cooper Marcus theorized that our experience of house and psyche are profoundly entwined. Thus (as Julia Morgan, herself, had) we often unconsciously create our home as a symbol of our persona. According to Cooper Marcus, designers unaware of the unconscious influence of their environmental autobiographies often recreate their own childhood places when designing for their clients. She recommended that place-makers unpack their environmental story to more consciously design based on their client's (not just their own) best-memories and emotions.

Cooper Marcus's words helped me realize that the fog I still kept stumbling through remained a fog full of messages and meanings inherent in my own environmental story. I went into therapy to see more clearly through that mist. I went looking for my full persona hidden beneath my childhood roof. It was time to move out from under there.

I moved to England where I met my future husband. I married, had a son and a daughter just as my mother had done, but I never just stayed at home. I became an associate professor at Hull School of Architecture where I was delighted to find other women teaching too. The School was committed to the architecture of social change. I began experimenting.

In my own Environmental Meaning course, I took my (mostly male) students through design *feeling* exercises that plumbed the depths of their past-place stories. Most of my students had working-class roots. Inevitably, as they dug deep into their pasts, they uncovered a gap—a divide between their own working-class background and the high-art culture espoused by the star architects they were meant to emulate. How could they reconcile the two worlds?

Rather than asking the students to discard their working-class origins, I encouraged them to intertwine their high-art architectural training with their memories of their lived experience—of light shining through lacy curtains or times spent sitting at grandma's cozy kitchen table. I encouraged them to uncover oft-forgotten primal memories of color, shape, texture, and space that had personal, emotional, or perhaps *transcendent* universal appeal. Such deep digging, psychological sifting, and re-constructing gave them permission to honor both their personal connection to place as well as their aesthetically oriented architectural education. By thus helping students uncover their lived experience (although I wasn't conscious of this at the time), I was trying to nurture connections and eliminate (not just theirs) but my own divides.

Then, abruptly, something happened that shook my Pollyanna presumptions about the school's openness. One day my school's dean ushered me into his office and closed the door. He announced that although I was the school's Overseas Liaison Officer, I'd no longer have contact with our Malaysian architecture students. The dean recently had visited Malaysia. When his Malaysian counterpart heard my last name was Israel (and that I was a woman, no less!), he "almost fell out of the cab" and insisted that I no longer work with the Malaysian overseas students.

Later, at our faculty meeting I mentioned this incident. No one said a word until the Head of Faculty remarked, "Tell them to take their students and go get stuffed!"[7] Someone defended me! So perhaps things had progressed since Morgan's time or, perhaps not. "Mysteriously," my liaison load was trimmed over the next few months. I considered raising the issue with the higher-ups but didn't want to make waves. Like Julia Morgan, perhaps I (and other women?) still feared that openly challenging the hierarchy would lead to paying a professional price.

Instead, upset that day, I simply left the building and said to myself, "I'm going home." After twelve years in England I decided to return to the U.S. This anti-Semitic incident coupled with my also having divorced made for a timely decision to return to the States.

Knowing somewhere in my heart that I still had things to share, I returned to America with my two young children and a book contract in hand, poised to write a book about the power of the psychology of design and the power of both opening and speaking up. Remembering that difficult journey, I wrote:

Under a foot big as a rock
I can't budge.
I squirm like a raw question mark
but questions lead
to possible answers
as I escape by
shrinking smaller, smaller until,
a dot, I bop across the ocean
to expand again
by the force of my own breath
drawn then released
like an exhale-mation point!
I am finally,
emphatically home.

Finding Your Woman's Voice

Perhaps *your* story contains fewer (or more) tales of a loved one who died too soon, or loss of a partner, or of a home. Maybe like Julia Morgan you are a designing-woman or another "other" who's had to overcome obstacles or repress your deepest self. Even if your life's tome includes less challenges, how do you claim (or reclaim) your powerful sense of self?

No matter who we are, each of our stories contains a psychological *subtext*—what renowned mythologist, Joseph Campbell calls the story of the "mythic journey of the soul."[1] Put simply, according to Campbell, the journey involves a hero who goes on an adventure and in a decisive crisis wins a victory, and then returns home changed or transformed. As described in his book, *The Hero with a Thousand Faces*,[2] Campbell explains that this archetypal hero's journey is really a "coming to consciousness."

Thus, understood as psychological *Circle of Life* quest, in Campbell's view, the hero moves along the path, then travels down deeply within, then steps back out from self-discovery's depths into the light of fuller self:

the hero is called to adventure, which they—or a loved one—resist. This is followed by some kind of aid from beyond their normal experience, the crossing of the threshold from known reality to an unknown world, an initiatory road of trials through the unknown, a big ordeal that results in ego-death and a new elixir, a return journey, struggle at the return threshold, resurrection of a new self, and the eventual delivery of the life renewing elixir, which redeems a wasteland.[3]

When Julia Morgan decided to become an architect, it was her call to adventure. As a woman trying to succeed in the design world, she faced many crises (trials) before developing her own successful practice. Her ordeal involved winding her way through a male establishment that put up barriers to her success. On the surface, one could say that her elixir was that she became a legendary architect who designed wonderful buildings for the world. Yet, did she really cross the threshold in the deeper psychological sense? Was she ever able to *return* to embrace, not repress, her full identity? After all, the hero's journey is a personal, emotional quest not a career or intellectual journey:

> *The whole idea is that you've got to bring out again that which you went to recover, the unrealized, unutilized potential in yourself. The whole point of this journey is the reintroduction of this potential into the world; that is to say, to you living in the world. You are to bring this treasure of understanding back and integrate it in a rational life. It goes without saying, this is very difficult. Bringing the boon back can be even more difficult than going down into your own depths in the first place."*[4]

Having gone down deep, when one does return to this fuller self, the rational and emotional self are integrated.

Interestingly, in her book, *The Heroine's Journey,*[5] therapist-artist-author Maureen Murdock suggests that there's a journey unique to women that's also a circular path to wholeness. In Murdock's view, however, women have the added challenge of overcoming the "wound of the feminine,"[6] the "myth of female inferiority"[7] as they struggle to make it in a man's world. She decries stereotyping that's persisted wherein, "Behaviors such as being active, independent, objective, and logical are equated with males, while more dependent, subjective, emotional and illogical behaviors characterize females."[8]

To heal the deep wound caused by such stereotyping, she believes that women must embark on "the quest to fully embrace their feminine nature, learning how to value themselves as women."[9] Of course, as in Julia Morgan's time, the existing culture may make it challenging for women to do so. Yet, according to Murdock, as the heroine overcomes obstacles and completes her journey, she integrates the so-called "masculine" and "feminine" side of her true nature.[10]

To achieve such personal evolution, she suggests, "The heroine must listen carefully to her true inner voice. That means silencing the other voices anxious to tell her what to do. She must be willing to hold the tension until the new form emerges. Anything less than that aborts growth, denies change, and reverses transformation."[11] As with Campbell's hero's journey, Murdock contends that, ultimately, the heroine's journey "is a very important inner journey toward being a fully integrated, balanced, and whole human being."[12]

Besides the "wound of the feminine," of course (as with my brief experience of anti-Semitism) there also exists the wound of the *other*, the message that one is inferior if they identify as something other than the culture's norm. To combat such marginalization, *Third Wave* feminism emerged in the early 1990s focusing on the crucial factors of race, ethnicity, class, religion, gender, and nationality. Third-wave feminists championed the *intersectionality* of women's experiences.

The hero's journey is a personal, emotional quest not a career or intellectual journey.

How do women who face othering not only stare down oppression but find their truest voice? Finding self-knowledge and self-integration isn't something most of us are taught how to do.

In the seminal book, *Women's Ways of Knowing: The Development of Self, Voice and Mind*,[13] four psychologist-authors offer further insight about how women come to know in the fullest sense. The authors interviewed 155 females from all walks of life—of different ages, class, ethnic, and educational backgrounds. As a result of these interviews, they identified five "Women's Ways of Knowing," which ranged from the powerless to the powerful including 1) Silence; 2) Received Knowing; 3) Subjective Knowing; 4) Procedural Knowing; 5) Constructed Knowing.[14]

. . . .

Women who were *silent* had no voice and were often young, poor, uneducated, and/or victims of abuse who often felt their voices unworthy. *Received knowers* looked unquestioningly to external authorities to provide the truth, which they believed resided outside themselves. Women who became more conscious, *subjective knowers*, began to question such gospel truth, realizing that a source of knowledge lay *within* them[15]—that their inner voice had worth. The idea of listening to their own voice, however, proved unsettling to these subjective knowers.

. . . .

I began to reflect on my lived experience as I read about these different categories. Thus my italics here are personal, I want to speak to you directly so you can feel not just think about your own transformation and finding your voice.

. . . .

When I was a young girl I wanted to believe that all was well. I said nothing and listened to doctors and relatives. "Everyone knows more than I do, don't they?" I didn't want to believe the truth that my father would leave this earth. Still, I knew what I saw—but I preferred to bury my doubts rather than bury my Dad.

. . . .

Women who moved further along the path became *procedural knowers* who questioned/challenged either by 1) separating and logically analyzing knowledge to determine the truth or by 2) connecting the knowledge they received, striving to understand how it was relevant to their lives and the lives of others.

. . . .

I was a teenager getting straight 'A's the year before my Dad's death. I knew how to nail those math tests and debate a fine point to the ground. My father died. Later in college, I read short stories at night to learn how others cope. I realized that, for me, there's little logic, just emotion when it comes to grief.

. . . .

Interestingly, most of the *separate knower* women were from traditional, elite, liberal arts colleges. They'd received A grades for learning to read words but hadn't yet learned to read their deeper world. While highly capable of critical thought, they worked hard to fit into the conventional education system that primarily values such impersonal analysis. *Connected knowers*, on the other hand, had to break free from traditional pedagogy to achieve a way of knowing based on feeling not just thinking. These latter women learned through empathy, the ability to truly hear and appreciate others' points of view.

. . . .

We heard stories of poverty and racism. I saw a photo of a naked orphan screaming, running down the street in Vietnam. We marched.

. . . .

Finally, then, often after deep self-reflection (and sometimes crisis), some women in the *Women's Ways of Knowing* study found their truest voice through *constructed* knowing—by integrating objective and subjective ways of knowing, by combining rational and emotive thought. From this perspective, those studied were able to engage in "*real talk*: the ability to listen, share and cooperate while maintaining one's own voice undiminished":[16]

Constructivists seek to stretch the outer boundaries of their consciousness—by making the unconscious conscious, by consulting and listening to the self, by voicing the unsaid, by listening to others and staying alert to all the currents and undercurrents of life about them, by imagining themselves inside the new poem or person or idea that they want to come to know and understand. Constructivists become passionate knowers who enter into a union with that which is to be known.[17]

Rather than "fit in," the role of design-heroines can be to champion the making of places that not only are beautiful or functional, but express and support positive change, growth, and sense of self.

When it comes to architecture, Karen Franck, likewise, discusses "Women's Ways of Knowing,"[18] identifying seven qualities she sees as typifying feminine or feminist ways of knowing and analyzing including:[19]

1. An underlying connectedness to others, to objects of knowledge, and to the world, and a sensitivity to the connectedness of categories;
2. A desire for inclusiveness, and a desire to overcome opposing dualities;
3. A responsibility to respond to the needs of others, represented by an "ethic of care";
4. An acknowledgment of the value of everyday life and experience;
5. An acceptance of subjectivity as a strategy for knowing, and of feelings as part of knowing;
6. An acceptance and desire for complexity;
7. An acceptance of change and a desire for flexibility

Of relevance in terms of Design Psychology, Frank goes on to cite the use of environmental autobiography as a strategy for uncovering subjectivity and feelings when it comes to making place. Apropos of Clare Cooper Marcus, she notes that such self/place storytelling can be a tool that raises designers' awareness about their own deeply held, environmental preferences.[20]

My architecture students certainly uncovered a trove of emotions, messages, and meanings in their past place treasure chests. Theirs were place riches—space, color, texture, and other sensory and environmental memories they then could embed in their designs. Thus, rather than design for "show," men as well as women can use their lived experience to discover, connect to, and design based on their most authentic self.

Overall, then, as the authors of *Women's Ways of Knowing's* also emphasize, the process of deeply knowing isn't necessarily a process exclusive to females. Yet the authors pose the possibility "that more women than men tip toward...*connected* knowing and more men toward *separate* knowing."[21]

As such, rather than "fit in," the role of design-heroines can be to champion the making of places that not only are beautiful or functional, but express and support positive change, growth, and sense of self. One interior designer, Randi Larowitz (a former singer), who I took through my Design Psychology exercises spoke about such transformation and self-expression in terms of her own making of place and self:

In this period of time now I'm ready to bring the singer back. I had to sublimate that to be Randi the designer. In the early part of my career I was designing for someone else—executing other people's designs. I was designing by what you learn is quote, "good taste." As you get more confident and secure you try to meld who you are, how to become the client, and what came before you historically in terms of good taste. Now I have to get myself out.[22]

I asked her what she meant by "get myself out." She explained by referring to wisdom passed on to her by an old acting teacher:

She used to say, "The only thing you have to bring as a creative person is yourself. You can't try to be someone else. If you are successful at art you bring yourself—everything else is meaningless." Getting myself out? I'm just at a point where my life has come full circle. I'm at the point where I'm confident enough to be able to say and express that.[23]

Has the culture shifted enough since Julia Morgan's time to allow other designing-women (as well as men) to embrace their full, most balanced voice? To find out, I met with an interior architect who navigated through tough, white male territory. Hearing the story of her unique lived experience, I soon learned how her brave journey resonated in her making of place.

Margo Grant Walsh

When Margo Grant Walsh opened the door to her Sutton Place, NYC apartment. I recognized her as the slender, striking woman with distinctive black glasses I'd seen featured in design magazines. Gracious, she put me at ease when inviting me into her entry foyer. It was the end of a long day for this woman who paved the way for women when she became the managing principal/vice chairperson of Gensler, a major commercial design firm often rated the number one design firm in the U.S. Inducted into the *Interior Design* magazine Hall of Fame in 1987, Grant Walsh has been described as "one of the most powerful and influential women in American architecture and interior design. She not only pioneered the way for woman in her field, but helped establish the profession as it is defined today."[1] She did this in a male- dominated corporate world.

Together Grant Walsh and I walked through her dimly lit hallway and sat down in her elegant living room with its deep red walls. Now, if you think I am going to recount to you the environmental autobiography of a high society, silver-spoon-in-her-mouth woman and thereby tell a story that obscures the "structural inequalities of Western society,"[2] you couldn't be more wrong. While Julia Morgan faced daunting challenges as a woman in architecture, Grant Walsh faced the intersectional obstacles of gender, class, and race. Nevertheless, she claimed her voice and power.

Once we sat down together, Grant Walsh's fascinating story didn't just tumble out. Her story emerged gradually as I took her through my Design Psychology *Toolbox of Exercises*,[3] by then a more formal version of the exercises I'd devised at Hull School of Architecture. Grant Walsh, born during the Great Depression (almost sixty-five years after Morgan), was alive and well before me. Thus, unlike Julia Morgan, I could interact with her by using the exercises from the Design Psychology Toolbox to explore the psychological foundation upon which her sense of place + self might rest. Thereby, too, I might gather further clues to see if this woman's way of knowing may have helped her achieve such success.

Grant Walsh began our conversation: "You may notice that my apartment is very dimly lit. That might seem strange to you. It seems very familiar to me. I grew up on a Native American reservation where there was no electricity so we lived by the dim light of candles."

As Grant Walsh completed my first *Environmental Family Tree* exercise, I learned about the very different branches of her tree. The daughter of a Scottish/Canadian mother and a Native American father, Grant Walsh was born on a Blackfoot Native

Margo Grant Walsh.
Photograph by Michael Maloney. Reprinted with permission *San Francisco Chronicle.*

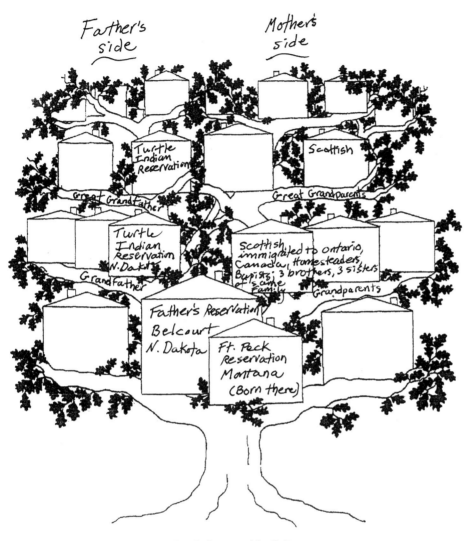

Father's side

Mother's side

Turtle Indian Reservation

Scottish

Great Grandfather

Great Grandparents

Turtle Indian Reservation N. Dakota

Scottish immigrated to Ontario, Canada, Homesteaders, Baptists; 3 brothers, 3 sisters of same family

Grandfather

Grandparents

Father's Reservation Belcourt N. Dakota

Ft. Peck Reservation Montana (Born there)

Your Environmental Family Tree

**Margo Grant Walsh's
Environmental Family Tree.**
Family Tree template drawn
by Sue Williamson.

American reservation in Montana and grew up in a Chippewa reservation in North Dakota. Such reservations were places of profound deprivation, lacking both electricity and plumbing. The only furniture the family owned was one green couch. Not only was the reservation a place of complete deprivation, it was a place of complete oppression. It was ruled with an iron hand by the Bureau of Indian Affairs and under their thumb no one had any say about anything.

Grant Walsh's mother, a schoolteacher in the reservation's one-room schoolhouse, wasn't paid. Instead she got "scrip" she could use in the company store. Her father delivered gravel, drove trucks, painted houses, and played in a local band. Interestingly, Grant Walsh's mother seemed to be the driving force in her family. Her father played the role of caretaker. She explained:

Mother was very disciplined. She must have been [my] model. I adored her grow-ing up. I also adored my Father. I never heard him say a bad word about anyone. He never gossiped about anyone. He was gentle. He was shy because he was Indian and looked Indian. Shy because of the reservation. They become very dependent.

My Dad was the family favorite because in 1918 when the great flu came through, he was the only one who didn't get it. He nursed all nine children—fed and washed his brothers and sisters. There was a goodness about him...

Besides the Bureau of Indian Affairs, the Catholic Church was the other insti-tution that dominated Grant Walsh's early life. She explained, "Every Indian res-ervation had a Catholic mission. I assume that the government invited the church in to convert the 'savages.' Yet, while many had bad feelings about the church, it had a positive association for me."

Grant Walsh and her family loved attending weekly services. She remembered the childhood excitement of buying a "bundle" at the church once a month:

Bundles in the Indian religion are sacred. Women volunteers would package them up...You could buy them and never knew what was in them. A pot, pan, or Indian beadwork...Indians were great designers and artisans. In the Plains, beadwork/ quillwork—we didn't put value on it. It was just what people did.

It was after church one day that Grant Walsh and her parents heard the news that would change both the course of history and her family's life: Pearl Harbor had been bombed. Like most Americans, her family was horrified by the attack. At the same time, Margo's mother's wheels were turning as she realized that the start of war represented an opportunity for the family to get off the reservation.

Shortly after the bombing, Grant Walsh's parents applied for and got jobs in the Portland, Oregon shipyards. The family moved to an Arts and Crafts bungalow. It was a step up—a symbol of the family's upward mobility and a step away from the oppressive policies of the Bureau of Indian Affairs. Reminiscing, Margo described that Portland home to me as "warm, cozy, comfortable, woody, and dignified."

From that nest, Grant Walsh had complete determination to make it in the world. She ascribed that determination to two messages she got from her mother: "Be successful to justify my marrying a Native American after being ostracized by the wider family," and, "Whatever you do, don't go back to 'the blanket'"—the blan-ket being the term for the Bureau of Indian Affairs/the reservation.

With those messages firmly implanted, Grant Walsh left home as a young adult with absolutely nothing, working her way through college doing a series of jobs. The only women in a class of men, she later graduated with an interior architecture degree in 1960.

After graduation, Grant Walsh began looking for a hard-to-come-by design job. Eventually a company hired Grant Walsh as a secretary, yet she also worked part-time doing renderings for Herman Miller, the renowned furniture company. Soon, however, they took one look at her portfolio, thought it was beautiful and asked, "Why are you a secretary?"

Determined to better herself, Grant Walsh finally got a design job in the interiors department of Skidmore Owings and Merrill's (SOM) prestigious firm. As she explained, it was a challenging place for women at that time:

It was definitely a man's club. The interiors department was buried because architects and designers didn't want us anywhere near them. Initially I was so self-conscious working with all of these men. They were architects and designers from Princeton and Harvard. I didn't worry about the male workers because I wasn't that attractive.

What I learned is very easy. You have to be useful. I just was smart and hardworking. I worked evenings, Saturdays. In those days it was a lot of Sundays as well. People used to ask, "Margo, why do you work so hard?" I'd say, "Look, I worked harder than this at school and I had to work to pay for school. Now I'm getting paid!" I think I got where I am today because I worked so hard.

Unlike Julia Morgan, Grant Walsh didn't try to mute her feminine identity. Things were different in Grant Walsh's era but still far from perfect. Male *clients* sometimes posed a challenge. Grant Walsh remembered one banker client who cornered her until she insisted, "Take your filthy hands off me." It was way before the #MeToo movement. Thus, later when she returned flustered back to the office, she told one of her colleagues what happened, begging, "Please don't tell the partners. I'm so embarrassed." Grant Walsh explained to me, "Early in my career, I learned never to let a client get familiar. I learned to be polite but not overly polite."

Although SOM appreciated Grant Walsh's hard work, she never got promoted and remained low paid after twelve years there. It was at this point that she was snapped up—hired by Gensler in 1973. SOM was surprised that Grant Walsh wanted to move on, saying to her, "Why didn't you ask us for a raise?"

Nevertheless, as Grant Walsh explained, the switch to Gensler was a wonderful career move:

I'd been held under a glass ceiling. [At Gensler] I could blossom. Even though I was surrounded by men at Gensler, the men liked me because I had skills. I grew into being more competitive and more aggressive. Determination. Hard work. Talent. I had great integrity. I was a leader. You can't teach a person to lead.

Once again, however, it was a male client who played a role in the most humiliating experience of her career. Asked to do a presentation to a Universal Pictures VIP, Grant Walsh went to J.C. Penney to buy the only suit she could afford. Later at the meeting, the V.I.P. looked at her and said, "I don't think I should buy this from anyone wearing a cheap suit. Just the way you're dressed tells me I shouldn't buy from you."

None of the others in the room defended her. They just said afterwards that they were glad she didn't cry. Explaining why she didn't cry, Grant Walsh continued telling me her story, "[I'd been] toughened up. My mother gave me that guts and gumption." She continued, "I still can't believe anyone could be that cruel. I thought, 'I'll show him!'"

And so she did. She started as a designer at Gensler but it became clear that her talents also lay in managing the design process. Marketing, mentoring, managing the office—she became the person *leading* the office. "The key was to listen, make decisions, define everyone's role clearly and...make sure everyone could always rise," Grant Walsh continued.

Although she also encouraged competition, she had a clear perspective on power. Grant Walsh could easily have followed the Bureau of Indian Affairs' abuse of power model. Instead, she too "ruled," albeit in the corporate design world, but did so with graciousness and modesty rather than follow the abusive model she saw on the reservation. She commented, "Everyone wants *power*—not sex or money, but power over time, over their life. But there's power and there's authority. I had a lot of power but I gave authority to other people. I always tried to be fair and straightforward. My door was always open."

As a powerful woman who took care to listen and delegate power, she combined what Marilyn Loden, author of the book *Feminine Leadership or How to Succeed at Business Without Being One of the Boys*,[4] described as "male" and "female" management styles:

Management Style	Male	Female
Operating Style	Competitive	Cooperative
Organizational Structure	Hierarchy	Team
Basic Objective	Winning	Quality Output
Problem-Solving Style	Rational	Intuitive/Rational
Key Characteristics	High Control	Lower Control
	Strategic	Empathetic
	Unemotional	Collaborative
	Analytical	High-Performance Standards

Interestingly, when I administered the *Personality and Place Exercise* to Grant Walsh, she scored as an ISTJ[5], an:

I = introvert who experienced the world based on
S = facts, analyzed things via a
T = thinking approach and preferred a
J = judging style, meaning preferring things clearly defined rather than open-ended

Her J trait may explain why she adopted a management approach wherein everyone's responsibilities were clearly spelled out. Overall, however, did Grant Walsh's *sensing* (fact-based) and *thinking* (objective) personality type make it easier for her to succeed in the objective, analytical world of architecture? What if she scored as an F (feeling) personality? What if she possessed more intuitive, emotional qualities? Would she still have been able to fit in and climb the corporate design ladder?

Regardless, since I score as a *Feeler* not just a *Thinker*, I was interested in examining ways Grant Walsh's moving *personal*, *emotional* journey may be linked to her home and corporate designs. When it came to her personal life, like Julia Morgan, Grant Walsh had little time to spare. She did, however, marry John Walsh when she was fifty-eight years old. She didn't regret her late marriage as Grant Walsh felt, "I married the man I waited for all of my life." Similarly, she didn't regret not having children as she never felt she would make a good mother.

Once married, she and John merged households, bought and renovated a dreamy Connecticut house, purchased a pied-de-Terre condo in Portland, Oregon, and kept her Sutton Place apartment. She seemed to have it all. Then her husband became sick with colon cancer and, sadly, died after they'd been married for only four years. By the time I conducted this first interview session with Grant Walsh, she had sold her Connecticut home, closing that chapter of her married life. She now lived full-time in the apartment where we sat. She'd spoken about these latter unfortunate events with sadness, but mostly with stoicism and a lack of self-pity.

Grant Walsh paused our conversation to show me around her two-bedroom apartment at this consummate Sutton Place address for those who've "made it." As we walked through its intense, warm, red rooms, the space felt as vibrant as Grant Walsh, herself. She mentioned choosing the red because it was the opposite of the drabness of growing up in a barren land.

In fact, she explained, "I was embarrassed by being a Native American and didn't want anyone to know. It came out in college when I applied to get a stipend." Grant Walsh hadn't tried to hide her feminine identity. Instead, she hid her ethnicity. In doing so, like Julia Morgan, she hid an important part of her self. Her home reflected such an image versus reality split since her front rooms exuded high-style and her back rooms were simple and modest.

As I looked around Grant Walsh's living room, for example, clearly it was the opposite of a place of deprivation. It was elegant, opulent, bold, and sophisticated. The room's wonderful oriental carpet complemented a beautiful oriental screen hanging over a cozy sofa against one deep red walls. Grant Walsh explained that the first oriental carpet she'd ever seen was one shown to her by one of her design professors. It became a symbol of the world of culture and sophistication she was about to enter as reflected in her gracious living room.

While her public rooms displayed her later success, her private bedroom and hallway spaces harked back to her modest roots. Against one wall in her back hallway was a sturdy, wooden Texas Primitive bureau. In her bedroom she had an Arts and Crafts Stickley dresser. All of these simple pieces were reminiscent of her family's warm, woody, dignified Arts and Crafts Portland home.

Margo Grant Walsh's Living Room, Sutton Place, NYC, 2001.

Photograph by the author.

Unlike Julia Morgan, however, Grant Walsh seemed in the process of melding her self/place divides. On the shelves in her living room were simple yet magnificent silver bowls and pitchers, part of her wider collection of Arts and Crafts silver. Contrastingly, displayed on the shelves were funky, wooden footstools—only a few of the four hundred she's collected. Why Arts and Crafts silver juxtaposed with wooden footstools? Perhaps these objects were touchstones unconsciously reminding her of the best of her past.[6] She elaborated:

My Father used to get glassware, dishes, and frames and refinish them. That's probably where I got collecting from— from my Dad. I started by going to flea markets. There I began buying the footstools. Although their basic footprint is the same, each is like a little work of art. They are all handmade. Someone designed and painted each one. They bring out the artist in the person.

Thus, in these deceptively simple footstools she could appreciate that there was something of value—of great worth. Similarly, over the years Grant Walsh began to realize that her Native American heritage wasn't something to be ashamed of, but equally of great worth. None of this symbolic connection was conscious. It wasn't something that occurred to her before we'd done the Design Psychology exercises. She remarked, for instance, "I never made the connection between my Arts and Crafts silver and the Arts and Crafts bungalow of my youth." Why would she make that connection since design training never considers the hidden, personal symbolism of place? Were Grant Walsh's silver bowls and footstools also unconscious talismans echoing to her to find and express her deepest self?

. . . .

A few weeks later I met Grant Walsh for our second session at Gensler's head office at Rockefeller Center in mid-town Manhattan. Sitting in the waiting room, I began to leaf through a book illustrating Gensler's corporate projects.[7] Since Gensler prides itself on being the "listening firm," rather than a firm of star designers, none of the book's case studies included any project designer's name. Nevertheless, I put a post-it by the photos of each project I guessed Grant Walsh, herself, had designed.

Once seated in her office, I showed Grant Walsh where I'd put the 10+ post-its. To her astonishment, each time I'd guessed correctly. I'd learned that once you begin to "read" the story of a place-maker's life, you can you see their story repeated in their public projects not just their private residences. Goldman Sachs' office with an oriental screen and silver tea set oozed the same sophistication as Grant Walsh's living room. King and Spalding's elegant waiting room in deep red with oriental carpets included the same high-class touchstones of success as in Grant Walsh's apartment. On the other hand, the David Polk and Wardell law office she designed was the essence of modesty and simplicity.

Explaining, I pointed out ways the high and low culture themes of her life were laced through these contrasting "high" and "low" corporate settings via the color, furniture, and special objects she'd chosen for each space. Clearly Grant Walsh was too busy to contemplate the intertwining of her sense of self and place. She was so busy, in fact, that she wasn't able to schedule a third and final Design Psychology session with me. This left some questions unanswered. Did her polar opposite high/low styles belie an unresolved tension between her private Native American identity and her hugely successful designer public persona? Which represented the authentic Margo Grant Walsh?

. . . .

Fourteen years elapsed before I re-approached Grant Walsh to complete our final session. By then she had retired from Gensler, yet embraced new challenges. Among them was co-authoring a book, *Collecting by Design: Silver and Metalwork of the Twentieth Century from the Margo Grant Walsh Collection.*[8] She also gifted portions of her silver collection to her alma mater, the University of Oregon, and to other museum collections. Those objects, many of which had been in storage—under wraps, so to speak—Grant Walsh now unwrapped like those exciting church bundles of her childhood. Both her public and private autobiographical riches were now available for all to see.

Similarly, in 2015 she curated an exhibit entitled *Adornment of the West: The American Indian As Artist* for the Buffalo Bill Center of the West in Wyoming. Included in the exhibit were Native American jewelry, beadwork, quillwork, and

Once you begin to "read" the story of a place-maker's life, you can you see their story repeated in their public projects not just their private residences.

Arthur J. Stone (American, born England, 1847-1938), Bowl ca. 1924-1936, sterling silver, 5 ¼ in x 8 1/8 in diam. The Margo Grant Walsh 20th Century Silver and Metalworks Collection.
Portland Art Museum, Portland, Oregon, 2002.91.11.

47 /

silver pieces designed and produced by Native American artists. Grant Walsh acknowledged the importance of displaying such work:

As a collector and connoisseur, I am drawn to American 20th-century silver both for its beauty, and for the heritage it represents. As artisans, American Indian artists are perhaps the single largest group in America to still maintain the European tradition of family apprenticeships, small shops, technical refinement, and innovation. And, through their artistry, American Indian silversmiths honor their own familial ties, tribal customs, and culture.[9]

Life comes around. Ultimately, Grant Walsh proudly embraced her Native American heritage and wrote these glowing words about Native American craftspeople.

In fact, when I went to Grant Walsh's apartment again for my third and final session with her, the biggest surprise was that her apartment walls were now a pleasant beige color—no longer painted bold red. "I wanted the beauty of my collections on these shelves to come to the fore," she remarked. The sophisticated silver, the footstools, the artwork were displayed prominently now with pride.

Overall, these beige walls were the backdrop for Grant Walsh to write her later chapter wherein she'd integrated and embraced her wonderful identity as both a sophisticated New Yorker *and* a Native American. In the end, then, Grant Walsh overcame obstacles as a female, minority place-maker, and broke barriers. By becoming a powerful woman she not only further empowered herself but, hopefully, inspires a sense of worth in both Native Americans and all designing-women.

Once Grant Walsh broke the glass ceiling, did other female place-makers find it easier to design their professional and personal lives in ways that made them feel whole? That's a whole other story which I'll continue now to tell.

"Buffalo Bill," a footstool from the collection of Margo Grant Walsh.
Photograph by Michael Maloney. Reprinted with permission *San Francisco Chronicle.*

CHAPTER 3:
Women on Fire

Igniting Design Psychology

I glance up and see geese flying against the blue sky in "V"ictorious formation. Did one generation show the next how to use their wings to fly? Victorious, Margo Grant Walsh, too, ascended great heights. I wish she'd been my mentor when I moved back from England to New Jersey in the early 1990s.

By then, environmental psychology had sparked interest, but hadn't caught fire since its founding in 1969. Architecture magazines still lauded beautiful buildings by (mostly male) starchitects. Universities courses rarely offered psychology courses along with design courses, despite calls for interdisciplinary learning. I wasn't sure what path to go down next.

Upon my return I was supposed to write a book about environmental psychology. "Personal Space," "Noise," and "Crowding" would be my worthy topics about this research field. Yet my fingers refused to type about those topics. Instead, I kept remembering back to ways I'd tapped into my students' memories of a warm kettle's whistle on a cold day, of slithering from rocky bank to pristine lake, of the scent of heather on hills. I felt sure it wasn't just a fluke that such echoes kept unconsciously reappearing in their designs. Such design elements seemed past-place signposts of those students' evolving self.

Then, too, apropos of my sessions with Margo Grant Walsh, I felt driven to uncover ways such environmental memories hidden beneath the surface, re-surface in the design of our homes and the spaces that even famous designers create. I felt certain that such insight could be *applied* to help professionals and all of us "design from within" our deepest selves. Grant Walsh found her self/home voice intuitively. Design Psychology might provide a method to do so *consciously* and, perhaps, more quickly.

Was my desire to write about using environmental autobiography as a catalyst when making place fueled by burning curiosity? By my own desire to heal my childhood wounds that kept forcing me to find how best to express authentic soul in space? Regardless, for months I dove into books by theorists who suggested ways to achieve a sense of wholeness. This led to my grounding Design Psychology in the well-known, classic theory of humanist psychologist Abraham Maslow who believed that we all can achieve a sense of wholeness and fulfillment via "self-actualization."

According to Maslow, self-actualized people are able to "appreciate again and again freshly and naively, the basic good of life with awe, pleasure, wonder and even ecstasy."[1] To reach this pinnacle of healthy selfhood, Maslow theorized that we have to satisfy a hierarchy of needs from 'physiological' to 'esteem' needs. For the purpose of Design Psychology I transposed Maslow's theory into a theory of

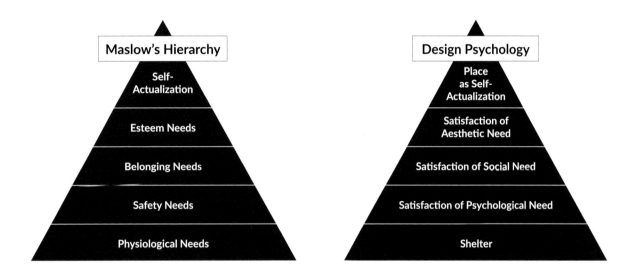

"Place as Self-Actualization":

According to the Design Psychology version of Maslow's hierarchy, to have a truly fulfilling place, one has to meet basic needs such as the need for shelter yet also meet psychological, social, and aesthetic needs. Typically, architects and interior designers necessarily are trained to focus on the bottom of the pyramid, i.e., shelter: buildings must stand up and the roof can't leak. They're also educated to focus on aesthetics. Often, however, the middle pieces—the emotional/psychological and social aspects of design are like less-valued (female?) children who've been left behind.

Alternatively, the actualized place-self pyramid offers a more holistic basis for design. With this in mind, each of the exercises in the *Design Psychology Toolbox*[2], like the *Environmental Tree Exercise* that I administered to Margo Grant Walsh, systematically explores and analyzes each level of the "Place as Self-Actualization" pyramid to assess if that client's environment is fulfilling. Yet this isn't simply a rigorous, objective process: apropos of women's ways of "knowing," it's a subjective, consciousness-raising process wherein the exercises subtly unfold not only one's past but one's present and future self/place story.

The Design Psychology Process

STEPS		EXERCISES
STEP 1	Explore past history of place.	Environmental Family Tree, Timeline, Guided Visualization, Mental Map Exercises
STEP 2	Identify positive associations with past place.	Environmental Family Tree, Timeline, Guided Visualization, Mental Map Exercises
STEP 3	Use positive associations to envision your ideal design.	Ideal Place Exercise
STEP 4	Climb the pyramid of needs to be satisfied to achieve ideal design.	Place Sociogram, Personality & Place, Homestyle, Special Objects Exercises
STEP 5	Using the pyramid as a touchstone, translate vision into final design.	Home as Self-Actualization Exercise, Design Psychology Blueprint

The Design Psychology Process has five steps encompassing the Design Psychology exercises to be completed. The exercises are meant to unearth one's environmental autobiography, which then serves as a touchstone for creating an *actual* new place.[3]

The point of going through the tools is to unlock people's visual images and sensory memories as well as patterns and messages received about their relationship to the world. Overall, then, the *Design Psychology Toolbox* acts as a key that unlocks each person's (often unconscious) treasure chest of environmental riches: sensory memories, feelings of *emotional* attachment to large- and small-scale settings, to dwellings, to furniture and to special objects.

The idea isn't for participants to engage in "nostalgia design"—to simply re-create idealized places from long ago. Then, too, when combing through the past, some places are best forgotten rather than recreated. Instead, via the Design Psychology process, one's environmental treasure chest is reworked to form a *Design Psychology Blueprint*, a written programming document, grounded in *positive* lived experience. The Blueprint recommends design elements—layout, colors, furniture, objects, etc., which, once translated into final design, act as catalysts helping clients to consciously envision and achieve self-actualization.

. . . .

I could have immersed myself forever in developing and writing about Design Psychology full time, but I had two young children (and myself) to support. Thus, while working on my book part-time, I found part-time positions in art, environment, and education non-profits where mostly women were employed. Inevitably such sincere and good work was satisfying but low-paid—a holdover from Julia Morgan's or my mother's time when (mostly women) worked as low-paid teachers or as unpaid volunteers? Sometimes, also, I discovered that my salary was less than my male counterparts.

Meanwhile, around this time, the *business* world had begun to embrace a new people-centered design approach that likewise acknowledged human emotions:

When empathetic design first appeared in business literature in the late 1990s, it was described as a cultural shift. Researchers in various disciplines hailed the importance of emotion as not only a valid subject of study, but as one that was crucial to design research (Dandavate et al., 1996). …Most significantly, the discipline was identified as a way to uncover people's unspoken latent needs and then address them through design (Leonard and Rayport, 1997).[4]

What sparked this new trend? Unbeknownst to me, there was a particular woman who helped pioneer people-centered design based in psychology. In the late 1980s to early 1990s psychologist Jane Fulton Suri began working as design director for the newly formed IDEO. Now arguably one of the most successful design firms in the world, IDEO first was known for their innovative product design.[5]

Fulton Suri, born in the 1950s to an artistic British family, early on acquired a sensibility for beautiful things. In her youth she imagined she would work for a trendy UK home and product chain. Yet, she later explained, "By the time I was in college, human psychology was more fascinating and then, applying psychology to architecture, could we design spaces and places to more intentionally support people?"[6]

After graduating from college, Fulton Suri worked for a decade as a human factors researcher and consultant specializing in consumer product safety. Then she met British industrial designer Bill Moggridge. Moggridge, the son of an artist, devised the first laptop computer. Thereafter, however, he realized that the physical form of the laptop was a very limited part of the experience and success of such a product.[7]

Moggridge and Fulton Suri together conceived of "Human Centered Design"— the creation of a physical and emotional dialogue between a person and a product, system, or service.[8] Did this *male* industrial designer and this *female* psychologist click because they had a mutual fascination with the emotional and psychological aspect of design?[9] Perhaps their artist-parent-mentors sparked a fire in each of them to champion human interaction as something the world needs in an ever-increasing technological society.

The Design Psychology Toolbox acts as a key that unlocks each person's (often unconscious) treasure chest of environmental riches: sensory memories, feelings of emotional attachment to large- and small-scale settings, to dwellings, to furniture, and to special objects.

In fact, although Fulton Suri was used to applying objective data to help in the design of products, at IDEO she drew upon deep-dive methods to understand the more qualitative lived experience of real individuals.[10] Tapping into the tools of environmental psychology, for example, she began "shadowing" users to observe their behavior. Likewise, she began interviewing—talking to users and hearing their stories, letting *empathy* guide her research. She came to see that such "design empathy" based on people's real-world experiences allowed for deep emotional understanding of their needs.[11]

Eventually Fulton Suri became an IDEO partner, playing a major role in infusing empathy into the company's design process. IDEO's projects expanded to include not just products but spaces "that empower communities, cities and even countries."[12] Throughout, guided by Fulton Suri, *storytelling* remained an intrinsic part of their design process. As IDEO's co-founder David Kelly remarked, "Jane fervently believes that her work is largely based on listening to and interpreting human stories. ...To her mind, it's about respect and humanity. Asking for a story celebrates and authenticates the experiences."[13]

Soon other companies like IDEO emerged and became the hot new thing along with new university interdisciplinary Design Thinking courses on human-centered design. Influenced by this trend, some architecture firms established in-house design research divisions to determine people's wants and needs when it came to place-making. Although not explicitly stated, such a shift by male-dominated design firms implicitly tipped further toward Franck's "women's way of knowing" in architecture in that it acknowledged the value of everyday life and experience as well as subjectivity and feelings as intrinsically important to design.

One such architecture, planning, interior, and design research firm hired me as a design research project manager. Once working for this firm, I collected data from online visual preference surveys like one that led to a new look for Las Vegas's downtown. I listened to participants' opinions during focus groups and interviews as they envisioned walkable, people-centered communities and homes from Trenton to Tennessee to Texas. Still, something was missing. Inevitably, what people say they *think* may be different from what they *feel* just below the surface. Did the data I was gathering really tell people's deeper stories as Fulton Suri's and my own "deeper than deep dive" method had done?

I considered such questions while finishing my book, *Some Place Like Home: Using Design Psychology to Create Ideal Places.* The idea of using one's environmental story and emotional inner life as the basis for design ignited interest. Major news outlets carried stories about the new field of Design Psychology as part of the movement toward more human-centered design. I began to speak to architecture and interior design groups, university programs, and at conferences in the U.S. and abroad to spread the word about Design Psychology.

All the while I continued working for the design/research firm run by men. I learned so much there but struggled to achieve a work/life balance as a 24/7 single parent. At least once I was advised not to pursue a management opening given my childcare responsibilities. When it came to women in the male-dominated architecture world, cultural shifts still had far to go. In the face of such challenges, I left that firm and created my own company[14] so that I could teach, write, research, and help people design from within on my own terms and flexible time.

Meanwhile, I kept receiving emails (almost always from women) like this one:

Dear Dr. Israel,
I have been in the architecture industry for 15 years and I have honestly lost my passion for it due to the lack of concern for the human element of design...I would like to change this. I am reaching out to you today in an attempt to gain insight into Design Psychology, advice on a path forward and any encouragement you can pro-vide as I navigate this new journey in my career. Can you tell me where I can study Design Psychology?
Thanks,
Lynda

Soon women almost weekly were emailing me to ask where they could study this new field. Eventually, to meet this need, I established my own online academia, offering Design Psychology webinars, workshops, and a mentorship program. That's when I noticed that most of those taking my courses and programs were female "NF" personality types[15]—what psychologist Carl Gustav Jung called "intuitive feelers." Such types process information by using empathy and imagination rather than just impersonal facts.

So, were more women than men interested in Design Psychology because it spoke to their expressive, inner selves? Were they doing so not just because of lack of equity or work/life balance struggles, but because they craved a missing piece: professional and personal self-integration?

If so, rather than see designing-women leave the profession, place-making organizations and institutions can help practitioners achieve such integration by including the psychological and social aspects of design under their umbrella. In the design world, when it comes to empathy, for example, as Fulton Suri et.al., point out there needs to be a *culture* shift, not just an individual mind shift:

to be most effective, empathy cannot remain the privilege of an individual, a design team, or even a tight group of highly involved stakeholders. Nor can it endure only for the course of a project. If design empathy is to sustain impact throughout an organi-zation, it needs ongoing support from the overarching culture. An empathetic attitude needs to be championed, nurtured, and practiced regularly...people within the organi-zation must learn to tell stories from an empathetic point of view and to ask for empa-thy when it's missing. Projects need understanding, enthusiastic champions who will tell and retell stories that keep empathy alive.[16]

"An empathetic attitude needs to be championed, nurtured, and practiced regularly... people within the organization must learn to tell stories from an empathetic point of view." – Jane Fulton Suri

Smoldering: Equity, Diversity, Inclusion, and #MeToo

In more recent days I've wondered, "Have such human-centered ways of being, knowing, and practicing place-making gained more ground? To find out, I wanted to hear (not just read about) how other designing-women were working and living their lives. Thus, one night I hopped across the Hudson River to attend the book launch for *Where Are the Women Architects?*[1] at the American Institute of Architects'(AIA) NYC headquarters. The book's author, architectural historian Despina Stratigakos, didn't speak about empathy or the need for psychological satisfaction in architecture. For her, the most pressing issue was to satisfy women's basic need for equity, diversity, and inclusion (EDI) in the profession. According to Stratigakos:

> *It seems like a case of historical or professional amnesia. The question of women's under-representation in architecture would be raised, followed by discussions about the challenges they faced and how to address them, and then the whole thing would be forgotten again. Then the cycle would be repeated, again and again, through the decades.*[2]

Stratigakos suggested ending the cycle of women's inequity "By knowing our history, finding allies to broaden the struggle, and using the power of new tools to raise and maintain awareness."[3]

She was speaking to the converted. One by one female architects who packed the audience rose to declare with smoldering frustration: "We deserve equal pay and promotions." "We need a voice at the table in terms of equal project opportunities." "What about basic professional respect?" Many also felt they had to work twice as hard and/or be extra-competitive to make it in the profession's male hierarchy. And…at what cost?

Manhattan high-rise, designed by Zaha Hadid, completed before her death.
Photograph by the author

Take Zaha Hadid, who in 2004 became the first female architect ever to win architecture's coveted Pritzker Prize. I'd approached her while I was writing *Some Place Like Home* to ask if she'd go through my Design Psychology exercises. At first she'd agreed but then backed off, saying "too busy."

Hadid, like Grant Walsh and so many women in architecture, felt she had to be competitive, tough, and hard-driving to succeed. Although Hadid "unmoored contemporary architecture from its affinities for right angles and male dominance,"[4] she did so at great personal expense. Hadid died of a heart attack at age 65. Her Manhattan skyscraper completed before her death[5] and her Miami high-rise finished after she died are monuments to her innovative, sensuous style. Yet they also could be read as super-sized tombstones with the epitaph: "Starchitect, died too soon from the stress of striving to be a successful woman in a man's world."

Writing about the uphill battles of such superwomen heroines, Murdock comments, "The boon of success leaves these women overscheduled, exhausted, suffering from stress-related ailments, and wondering how they got off-track. …The image they held of the view from the top did not include sacrifice of body and soul."[6]

In fact, in 2017 an American Institute of Architects' "Equity, Diversity, and Inclusion Commission" reported these survey findings by the AIA and other groups:[7]

- Women and minorities are under-represented in the profession.
- Aligned with the perceptions on representation of women, half of the surveyed women respondents report that women are less likely to achieve their career advancement objectives.
- Women and minorities say they are less likely to be promoted or compensated at rates equal to their peers.
- Minorities reported that their barriers to entering the profession included fewer education financing opportunities; a perceived low "return" on the expense of schooling; a lack of role models; and low awareness of career paths.

To find out if and how designing-women cope with such challenges, I attended other women-in-architecture gatherings like the 2017 AIA Women's Leadership Summit in Washington, DC. I expected to find its 400 female attendees smoldering there, too. To my surprise, although equity, diversity and inclusion (EDI) remained a vital thematic undercurrent, each presenter told her interwoven *personal* as well as professional tale—ways they'd constructed their self as well as their buildings. Such stories of these women's lived experiences were so different from the usual "show and tell" format of traditional architecture conferences that focused on latest projects.

Instead, although no speakers at this Summit explicitly referred to Campbell, Murdock, Franck, or *Women's Ways of Knowing*, each had walked the path: a "call to adventure," "trials," "flight," and final "return," as well as the journey to overcome that "wound of the feminine." Telling and listening to one another's stories enabled them to connect and find their professional and personal, human voice.

Two years after this DC gathering, almost a thousand assembled for the next Summit.[8] It was the largest meeting of women architects ever held in the U.S. up to that point. Participating in that gathering, I realized that (perhaps subtly) a trend toward a more balanced way of being when it came to place-making really might be taking place. Although together in huge meeting rooms, it was as if the Summit's female architects born anywhere from Siberia to Nigeria were sitting around glowing campfires bonding—trying to "shift their identity through transformational conversation."[9] Why do that?

"To be integrated is what we should all be striving for," remarked Julia Gamolina, a Summit speaker and editor of *Madame Architect.org*, a website "about women putting their narrative and their story at the forefront, and about giving them a voice and a platform."[10] In answer to "Where are all the women architects?" Gamolina proclaimed, "They are right here!"[11] The website, founded by Gamolina in 2018, has featured over three hundred and fifty stories of female architects, at last count.

More recently, in fact, there's been a feminist *Fourth Wave*. As with the other feminist waves, this fourth one is not easily defined. Some say it began 2012 when women started to claim their power through the news media, especially via the internet's social media platforms. Online features such as those in *Madame Architect.org*, for example, have raised awareness about the increasing number of females becoming architects as well as heads of design firms and university design schools/departments. Then, too, social media allows women not only to highlight issues around equity, diversity, and inclusion but to very publicly point to "power abusers" including via formats like #MeToo that call out sexual abuse/violence against women.

Although encouraged by such advances when it comes to women's issues and women's ways of knowing, I couldn't get complacent once I heard Angela O'Byrne, FAIA's speech at the Women's Leadership Summit. It raised my awareness about how much further all women—not just designing-women, have to go to achieve basic human rights. The autobiographical story of O'Byrne's rise to become president of Perez, a 100% women and minority-owned New Orleans architecture firm, was an inspiration. Her speech (abbreviated below) brought to life the everyday peril and oppression her Afghan interns and women around the world face that urgently need to be addressed.

"Women on Fire" by Angela O'Byrne, FAIA[12]

I was born in Cali, Colombia, SA, in 1960—the fourth girl in a culture that values sons over daughters. My parents received condolences that yet another girl was born. Thankfully, my parents did not subscribe to that type of thinking and my father always treated us the same as he treated our only brother.

The country where I was born is Third World poor. Though somewhat educated, both my mom's and dad's families were poor. My mother never went past high school. Out of his eight siblings, only my father and one other went to college, paid for by their siblings who pooled their resources to send the two brothers to university.

Father moved us to the U.S. when I was five years old. He took a position as a professor and researcher at Tulane University Medical School. He instilled in us a love of learning and an interest in education and the arts including music and architecture. We all received exceptional educations, the best that our parents could afford. We girls were never "less than" any boy.

I finished high school in 1978 and promptly got married shortly after my 18th birthday. I had three children in rapid succession, two of them while I was an architecture student. My mother and the dean of the School of Architecture both predicted I never would finish college. I finished with honors, getting Best Thesis Project. Then I had my third child; no one ever tells men that their lives will end, because they have children. Lesson learned: Believe in yourself, because sometimes nobody else will.

In 1987, after getting my Columbia degree, I worked for a housing bond issuer on Wall Street. I moved to northern New York State because my husband did not like city living. I lived there for five years. During that time we divorced and he returned to New Orleans. Eventually, the children followed Dad to New Orleans. I could not find a job there so I returned to NYC to work at SOM, Gensler, and AECOM. I commuted to New Orleans to see my children every other weekend and continued seeking a job in New Orleans. During those very difficult years, my parents were very supportive. At one point my mom said something that we should say to all women going through difficult times: "You are not just a mother or a wife. Your life has value. You must find another reason to live. You must get up and start over." After six years of commuting from NYC to New Orleans, Perez hired me in 1998, allowing me to be closer to my children.

As part of the firm's work for USAID, the projects are all social impact projects like clinics, hospitals, schools, and universities. Our contracts actually also require that we do Gender Capacity Building in the case of our work in Afghanistan. I was worried about our ability to deliver this part of the contract. I was worried that my older male Afghan engineers would not take this part of our contract seriously.

Much to my surprise and delight, Perez's older male Afghan engineers hired the few young female grads in Architecture/Engineering/Accounting. We have three new ones every semester and we keep a few full-time after they graduate. Right now we have three female full-time graduates.

Angela O'Byrne, FAIA (center right) with interns Bibi Khaironnessa Hashemi (far left), Humaira Latifi (far right), and Maryam Shams Ansari (center left).
Photographer unknown.

It does feel good to know that we are able to give young Afghan women paying jobs that allow them to obtain much needed experience in design, construction, and accounting, and to put their education to good use in their communities. They battle so much, just to get to school in the first place—their fathers must be very supportive, more so than their mothers because the mothers really have no say. When these Afghan women graduate there are no jobs for them, as women. The jobs go to the men. So, my firm has been able to engage women architects from their home country (in this case Afghanistan) to be able to:

Design build 200 bed women's dormitory, American University of Afghanistan (AUAF), designed by Perez APC; Client: USAID.

Photograph by Technologists Inc.

1. Have gainful employment in their chosen field in an environment that is often hostile to women

2. Work with women clients for women and family centric government agencies to provide buildings to house schools, health clinics, etc. That really makes a difference for women and children.

Another example of the plight of women in Afghanistan: We recently completed the renovation of fire code-related work in a girl's high school, the Sardar Kabuli Girls High School. The principal at the end met with me at the school and I later invited her to lunch at my office compound. Both times she cried and said the girls were routinely kidnapped and murdered on their way to and from school. She is in her seventies but does not retire as she is devoted to the mission of teaching the girls and I imagine they have a tough time recruiting teachers. The school was meant for 2,000 girls, but housed 7,000 in three daily shifts—many of the rooms don't have desks, so they sit on the cold hard terrazzo flooring. Perez's Afghan partner company donated desks and chairs to the school to fill the remaining rooms that lacked furniture.

Each time that I go to Afghanistan, I take time to eat lunch with the young female interns and I tell them my life story. Then I listen to theirs. You can hear a pin drop. They hang on every word and, of course, I am very interested in hearing what they have to say. It's very moving to me. They say things they would never say in front of the men. Sometimes they sing, recite poetry, etc., for me in their language, though I don't understand. The Taliban forbids music and poetry and literature so even when they do this, they look over their shoulders fearfully to make sure no one outside of our little circle is listening.

Sometimes I give classes to both the men and the women on project management, marketing, design, and technical matters, Building Codes, etc. They hang on every word, so eager to learn, thirsty for knowledge. I imagine the class will be one-hour long and it turns into three hours because they have so many questions.

After doing this work, when I come back to the U.S. and hear my staff complain about anything, I think—"you aren't homeless, starving, or living in a war zone—what could be so bad?" There have been days when bombs one kilometer away shook my office compound, windows broke, and I had to go outside fifteen minutes later and walk to the U.S. Embassy where we had a client meeting that did not get cancelled despite the bomb. The thought of Perez's Afghan staff's work, occurring under threat of fire, either as a collateral of a military presence or as a threat from their own community's cultural stigmas, makes the Perez U.S. staff so grateful that we don't have to face these threats in our daily experience just to be able to do our job.

In a way, my firm's work in Afghanistan makes our complaints in the U.S. may seem small by comparison with those of women in other countries—but it really is about all women worldwide, striving to move forward in our profession to the highest level possible. Believe me, women in the U.S., including women architects, serve as role models for the women of other countries who are, in some cases, far more oppressed than we are. It is because we do and will continue to progress forward in the U.S. That right there is hope for women in more oppressive countries.[13]

. . . .

O'Byrne, brave, competitive, driven, empathetic, compassionate, and inclusive, parlayed her persona in ways that challenged the oppression of women. By sharing her lived experience with them and by listening deeply to their women's stories, she offered her young interns emotional safe-passage (albeit momentarily).

O'Byrne's interns risked their lives just to sing and recite poetry with her. Clearly such artistic expression served as the interns' creative, psychological protection—emotional armor—as necessary for survival, perhaps, as any bodyguards or armored cars. This is testimony to O'Bryne yet also to the power of creative expression, including the art of telling one's own story, that such expression helped them (metaphorically at least) to transcend—to journey in their mind, out of fire. Thankfully I'm not in Afghanistan. I'm privileged here for years now in America. In truth, although most of us are not under machine gun fire, for all of us there is that slow fire—that ember of fully expressed self, hidden behind the smokescreen of daily life. That ember must be tended to fuel our souls. Yet is it enough to use Design Psychology to create soul-filled poetry in spaces when women struggle to be free in actual places? A chart showing the the *Four I's of Oppression* that I came across helped me answer that question:

Although most of us are not under machine gun fire, for all of us there is that slow fire— that ember of fully expressed self, hidden behind the smokescreen of daily life. That ember must be tended to fuel our souls.

The Four "I's" of Oppression[14]

Ideological Oppression
when one group believes that they are somehow better than another and that they have the right to control the other group.
Institutional Oppression
when the ideology that one group is better than another gets embedded in the institutions of the society such as its legal, educational, or hiring systems.
Interpersonal Oppression
when individual members of the dominant group personally disrespect or mistreat individuals in the oppressed group.
Internalized Oppression
when oppressed people, themselves, come to believe in their own inferiority.

I could see how the first three overlapping I's of Ideological, Institutional, and Interpersonal Oppression had undermined Angela O'Byrne and her interns as well as Julia Morgan, Margo Grant Walsh, and the many women whose tales I'd heard. The impact of Internalized Oppression, however, is sometimes more difficult to discern although just as toxic.

When it comes to architecture, for example, architect/urban planner, firm head, and alternative architecture school[15] founder Odile Decq comments:

> *I often talk to female students in the school and encourage them to be more self-confident. This is a problem women often have: not being self-confident enough to trust themselves to be able architects. ...women often doubt their ability to succeed. It is a question of education, from their family and from the society around them. Mothers too often love their sons and ask their daughters to help them. Fathers too often admire the beauty and docility of their daughters while praising the strength and courage of their sons. It's a shame the starting point is not equal. I continue to observe these patterns even with young, modern couples today![16]*

I knew just what she meant. Although I, too, had my scrapes with all the I's, it was Internalized Oppression that most pulled me down. Despite Design Psychology's success, a little voice in my head kept insisting that I wasn't good enough. At first I thought the fog I felt was gray remaining grief. But mine were upbraids about what I "should," "ought," and "must" wear, or say, or do to be a woman of worth. I lacked self-esteem.

Therapy raised my awareness about my own story—about ways my internal critic was repeating critical voices I'd heard in the culture around me and in my childhood home. Such insight helped me bring my lived experience to the surface and pinpoint the problem. But how could I solve it? Shining a light on any problem is a crucial initial step. Then, too, a circle of empathic friends, wise mentors, and hearing the stories of others' journeys all helps.

I realized that in the end when it comes to place-making and sense of self, Design Psychology also provides an antidote to such internalized oppression by acting as a catalyst for self-love and self-esteem. The Design Psychology process helps silence dictates about how we as well as our space should, ought, or must look or be: *Designing from within* as authentic expression rather than for show, acts as a *liberating* type of design. Like those Afghan intern's soulful songs, it helps ignite our sense of self and soul. As feminist theorist/writer Bell Hooks reminds us:

> *The more we accept ourselves, the better prepared we are to take responsibility in all other areas of our lives...Taking responsibility does not mean that we deny the reality of institutionalized injustice. ...Taking responsibility means that in the face of barriers we still have the capacity to invent our lives, to shape our destinies in ways that maximize our well-being."[17]*

With all of this in mind, I want to tell you the story of another designing-woman who experienced all of the "I"s. A legend in our time, she spoke out and made places in ways that battled oppressions, moved women forward, and helped her achieve her own self-esteem.

Denise Scott Brown,
RIBA, Int. FRIBA, Hon. FAIA

One autumn at twilight, I headed to the home of Denise Scott Brown,[1] the first *living* female ever to win the
American Institute of Architect's Gold Medal. This ar-
chitect/planner together with her husband Robert Venturi helped pioneer postmodernism, a movement that
opened up opportunities for marginalized groups to express their diversity[2] rather than hide difference.

Scott Brown, too, experienced the "wound of the
feminine." She was well aware of the discrimination
she faced as a "woman architect." In *Room at the Top?
Sexism and the Star System in Architecture*, Scott Brown
wrote passionately about the sexism she experienced:

> *My stories include social trivia as well as grand
> trauma. But some less common forms of discrimina-
> tion came my way when, in mid-career, I married a
> colleague and we joined our professional lives just as
> fame (though not fortune) hit him. I watched as he was
> manufactured into an architectural guru before my
> eyes and, to some extent, on the basis of our joint work
> and the work of our firm.[3]*

She rightfully balked at instances when her contribution was overlooked or
when she felt she was the token woman at the table. In *Room at the Top*, Scott Brown
describes the consequences of speaking up:

> *my complaints make critics angry, and some have formed lasting hostilities against
> both of us on this score. Architects cannot afford hostile critics. And anyway I begin
> to dislike my own hostile persona.*

> *That is when self-doubt and confusion arise. "My husband is a better designer than I
> am. And I'm a pretty dull thinker." The first is true, the second probably not. I try to
> counter with further questions: "How come, then, we work so well together capping
> each other's ideas in both design and theory? If my ideas are no good, why are they
> praised by the critics (even though attributed to Bob)?[4]*

Such oppressive practice was enshrined in 1991 when Robert Venturi alone was
awarded the coveted Pritzker Prize for architecture rather than the award going to
both of them. Despite this, Scott Brown recommends to female architects, "Don't
do the work because you want to get a prize. I didn't go into architecture because I
thought I might get a prize."

Denise Scott Brown.
16th Street Office, c. 1968,
Photographer unknown.
Courtesy Venturi,
Scott Brown and Associ-
ates, Inc.

**Freemont Street,
Las Vegas, NV.**

Photograph by Denise Scott
Brown, 1966. Courtesy Venturi,
Scott Brown and Associates,
Inc.

*By embracing
differences in lived
experience, Denise
Scott Brown enabled
people to express
themselves while
also breaching
divides.*

. . . .

I got my first hint of the multi-faceted story of this design-heroine I was about to meet when driving though Scott Brown's suburban Philadelphia neighborhood. A mixture of historic stone houses stood next to decrepit neighborhood shops. Her block, lined with 1950s split-levels, seemed surprisingly *under*whelming. Yet at the road's end sat her Art Nouveau mansion, a gracious, stone, commanding presence. More curious juxtapositions soon followed.

I arrived to find Scott Brown at her door—warm, welcoming, gray haired—dressed appropriately in a cozy gray sweater and...huge, bright yellow Mickey Mouse slippers! I laughed silently, trying to be respectful as I walked into her home.

At first I thought Scott Brown might have lost it when she greeted me in her eye-popping slippers. It rapidly became clear that they were signs of her wit. Denise Scott Brown at eighty-six was not only an engaging, brilliant woman but still as sharp as a bright neon tack. I sensed she'd have a lot to say since, like Julia Morgan and Margo Grant Walsh, she was a pioneer.

I'd been one of her worldwide admirers ever since visiting the *Signs of Life: Symbols in the American City* exhibit[5] in DC in 1976. As with *Learning from Las Vegas,*[6] the landmark book that she'd co-written, the exhibit lauded diverse, design-in-everyday-life rather than "high-art" architecture. To many Americans, Las Vegas's glaring neon advertisements seemed so commonplace, even kitsch. Scott Brown, however, was raised in South Africa so she viewed the Strip differently. Looking through her foreigner's lens, she deemed that neon part of everyday vitality—a unique sign of American life. In glorifying the Strip's neon-scape, the *Signs of Life* exhibit helped set the scene for diverse, expressive postmodernist architecture—a radical departure from minimalist, modernist white.

For years I found her approach provocative. After all, in my work with my British students, I recognized how their different forms of cultural expressions often seemed to collide with accepted norms. Where America was concerned, Scott Brown observed:

The United States is a diversified nation, differentiated regionally and ethnically, stratified socially and culturally pluralistic; yet it is also a mass society that shares symbols and systems to such an extent that Americans are accused by outsiders of being a nation of conformists.[7]

By embracing differences in lived experience, Denise Scott Brown enabled people to express themselves while also breaching divides. How did she come to adopt this stance? While on her path, how did she discover and use her unique designing-woman's voice? My goal was to find out by taking her through my exercises.

Scott Brown, friendly, self-assured, and with a mischievous smile, ushered me inside. I wondered what the interior of their home possibly could look like, given that she and Venturi had upended the sterility of late modernism. I quickly realized that their home's decor was the opposite of a white, min-imalist shrine.

I walked with her into their large, cozy living room. *This* was no sterile stage set. It brimmed with a hodgepodge of pop-art pillows, paintings, a piano, and *objet-d-art-nouveau* furniture.

Before we sat down she suggested, "Look out the windows at that sunset. Part of why I bought this place was because of the expanse, the lookout over the garden. In Africa I had that kind of view."

Denise Scott Brown's and Robert Venturi's home, Philadelphia, 2008.
Photograph by Mark Sfirri, Courtesy Venturi, Scott Brown and Associates, Inc.

As soon as we sat down, her multicultural story unfolded as she completed her *Environmental Family Tree*. Born in Zambia in 1931, Scott Brown was two years old when she moved to South Africa where she was raised. Tracing back, however, it became clear that her past-place roots were also European, since her ancestors were poor European Jews living in shtetls.

Scott Brown's Grandmother Becky, in particular, was a strong female ancestor who, like Scott Brown, overcame obstacles to make her way in the world. Becky was born to Jewish parents in a poor, little Latvian town. This family lived in "wonky," "crazy" wooden houses constructed by the people who lived there. Orphaned early, Grandma Becky was raised by nice, solidly middle-class relatives in the capital city of Riga. This grandmother was very beautiful with her hair pulled back in an Art Nouveau style. "Like someone out of a Klimt painting," commented Scott Brown explaining that Becky dressed in a distinctive Art Deco style, "She imagined her-self a grand lady."

In 1903, Becky became a mail-order bride who moved to Zambia to marry her hus-band Winnie. Before long, Becky was wearing an apron, cooking over a three-legged stove in the wilderness, sewing, and making do. Eventually the couple built a mud-thatched house where they lived a life of cultural cross-pollination: inside the house they had a piano. Becky served tea in a teapot as a very English lady would. Outside were lions everywhere. In fact, Scott Brown's mother played in the wilderness with little animals yet had a French governess—"as any elegant lady from Riga must," Scott Brown quipped wryly. Upwardly mobile, that family then moved to a lovely, typical Johannesburg house.

Denise Scott Brown's parents grew up in more well-established house-holds among a swirling mixture of Jewish, European, and African influences. Interestingly, her mother became an architect. In those days in South Africa, female designers appeared to have the same rights as men. Thus, Scott Brown's mother didn't need to hide her feminine identity as Julia Morgan needed to do in her time and place.

In fact, Scott Brown's mother had a unique sensibility that profoundly influenced her:

My mother used to take us walking in the veld, [expansive, open countryside in South Africa]. Her governess took her to the veld and taught her how to make music out of any leaf you could find. She taught her how to make floating boats out of walnut shells. My mother was a hive of information about handicraft...She often drew houses, children and even cars for us, saying, "Here's how a car will look one day." Later when we saw a Volkswagen van I said, "Oh, the house my mother drew!"

Denise Scott Brown's child-hood home, Johannesburg, South Africa, by Hanson, Tomkin, and Finkelstein, designed 1934, built 1935, now demolished.
Photograph 1957 by Denise Scott Brown. Courtesy Venturi, Scott Brown Associates, Inc.

Completing her *Environmental Family Tree*, Scott Brown explained there was this "big break" in terms of home patterns because of her mother's keenness for modern architecture. She reminisced about the Johannesburg international-style family home where she lived from ages four to twelve:

That house was my mother's loving intention for it and for us. It was my father's somewhat puzzled but very amused acquisition. It had a flat roof which was very unusual. It was beautiful but it also was functional. When I was a little kid, I went up the stairs and when I got to the half-landing I swung my body around and I went in a half-round circle...There's a lot of happiness in all that...

It was a delightful childhood image that Scott Brown relished recalling. Likewise she recalled nostalgically, "There was a little window in the east where you could go out and look at the sun. . ...My mother would do that every morning and say, "It's going to be a lovely day today."

A woman greeting another female by showing her light—no wonder when we first entered her living room, Scott Brown welcomed me by pointing to the soft-setting sun. In fact, she observed, "There is one view between the fir tree on the left and the German linden on the right. I call it my "bush veld" because in the winter it reminds me of the low-lying [South African] bush-veld."[8]

In a later *Place Timeline Exercise*, she observed that both her family's South African modernist house and her present Philadelphia home, built in 1907, were her favorite residences and had a similar house-large yard relationship. Her home's view and setting were echoes of her childhood experience of place.

Denise Scott Brown and Robert Venturi's Philadelphia home (Exterior view).
Photograph by Denise Scott Brown

She commented further, "I fell in love with this house instantly [and] said, 'I can't believe there's an Art Nouveau house in America!'" Yet, like Grant Walsh's apartment, Scott Brown's current home seemed to reflect two opposite design sensibilities—each an imprint from her past. On the one hand, her home's elegant Art Nouveau/Art Deco style was as European as her grandmother's hairstyle and dress. Structurally, on the other hand, the house's simple, rectangular shape repeated the form, the timeless *essence* of her mother's international-style Johannesburg house. Scott Brown explained:

> *For me, the notion of [this house] was Art Deco—and international style more than Art Deco because of its grandness and simplicity. You see, if I hadn't found this, I'd be looking for a house that had the timeless industrial quality that the modernists liked and that my mother liked.*

Denise Scott Brown
and Robert Venturi's Home,
Philadelphia, 2008.
Photograph by Mark Sfirri.
Courtesy Venturi, Scott Brown
and Associates, Inc.

As she continued, there seemed to be other echoes from her childhood that might explain why Scott Brown chose this house. In her youth she certainly got the message that "better" ladies should live in "better" houses. Grandma Becky also always told her about the "so beautiful" Art Nouveau houses in Riga. Scott Brown continued, "Our family had some rickety and some grand houses. With my grandmother [Becky], it wasn't upward mobility—it was vertical take-off! It was real poverty. She went to school hungry in the morning and she ended up a lady living with more fashionable people."

Then, too, Scott Brown had a "very, very famous" uncle in Oxford, a professor in England, who lived in a beautiful Art Nouveau house. She admired the fact that he was not just "probably very well off" but "intellectual and cultured and having the ability to live a cool life." Did Scott Brown choose her current house because it unconsciously symbolized similar aspirations she had for her own life/self?

Certainly upward mobility was a deeply ingrained family theme. The messages Scott Brown received about bettering oneself weren't subtle. When her family moved to their modernist South African home, for example, one relative commented, "Don't worry, you'll soon be going 'up the hill.'" Not surprisingly, then, Scott Brown repeated this message to me commenting, "Part of what you want for your children is to be upwardly mobile."

Yet simply moving to a grander home doesn't ensure a grander life. As I dug more deeply into Scott Brown's environmental story, it became clear that the international-style house of her youth held both fond as well as challenging memories and emotions for her. Scott Brown explained that she lived in that cool, white house during South Africa's Great Depression of 1936 when:

> *My Dad was a very worried and irritable man and we were scared little children...I kind of took my Mother's side as she was the one that sponsored the house. ...It was also [a way of] saying that there's some protection and happiness around this house even though my Dad was so black.*

Hôtel du Département de la Haute-Garonne, Toulouse / Two dimensional columns representing a monumental entry in Toulouse's historic tradition, Hôtel du Département de la Haute-Garonne, Toulouse, France, 1999, designed by Venturi, Scott Brown and Associates, Inc. in association with Anderson / Schwartz Architects and Hermet-Blanc-Lagausie-Mommens / Atelier A4
Photograph by Matt Wargo. Courtesy Venturi, Scott Brown and Associates, Inc.

Her father:

was subject to towering anger and scary as hell. We had to be like little mice on certain days when we saw the atmosphere around him. It made me very suppressed...And I had a mother who was pretty neurotic, so she couldn't stand up against that, she was just scared of it."[9]

Thus, I wasn't convinced that Scott Brown ever would have settled happily in America in a purely industrial-style, modernist house: her South African modernist home had too many negative, not just positive, overtones for her. Glancing again around Scott Brown's living room, the eclectic décor and the pluralistic style she championed all seemed to me to be a turning away from much of what her modernist childhood home symbolized. You might think I'm speculating here. All designers have past-place stories yet ground their work in history, theory, and their own aesthetic. Ah, yes, but design psychologists have insights regarding ways a person's environmental autobiography may unconsciously influence their sense of place and self. It's my "way of knowing" and my job as a design psychologist to make such connections. Thus, I wanted to understand what other childhood place influences may have had an impact upon Scott Brown.

Scott Brown herself recognized the importance of childhood place, commenting, "My first early memories have been very, very influential on me. Rather than saying, 'What did Corbusier do?' one should ask, 'What do I remember and what things affected me?'"[10] Amazingly, she could remember all the way back to being on site with her parents when she was two years old as they held up working drawings for a house they were building. She had other *sensory* memories, too:

I remember the odor of the gum tree (eucalyptus tree), the eucalyptus oil—and orange blossoms, a sentimental smell—and the smell of wild and cultivated flowers in the yard, the mignonette—and the smell of the veld, fresh and wonderful, and the smell and taste of fruit—peaches, plums, oranges, grapes in particular, everything you can imagine.[11]

In 1944, when Scott Brown was twelve, her parents moved from the modernist house to an expansive North Western Johannesburg suburb—"upper middle-class territory." Seen through my lens, this move appeared not only personally formative for Scott Brown, but formative in terms of her famous work. "This next house," she explained, "was on three acres, designed by a well-known Johannesburg architect and modern like a Frank Lloyd Wright house but bigger." Yet living in an upper middle class, *physical* place didn't obliterate the other emotional/social challenge she faced there: anti-Semitism. Without bitterness, yet with clarity, Scott Brown recalled:

[My parents] put us in private schools which meant the other Jewish children didn't have much to do with us nor would the Christian children. [The private school] was mostly Christian. Those girls were very anti-Semitic. They didn't ask us to their parties and the Jews kept to themselves, too.

Such anti-Semitism wasn't confined just to Scott Brown's local community. She remembered:

Ndebele houses, Mapoch Village, South Africa, 1957. Photograph by Denise Scott Brown. Courtesy Venturi, Scott Brown and Associates, Inc.

When Hitler started, I had all sorts of fears as a seven year old. During the War he said he was going to come to Johannesburg. I remember coming to sit with my grandmother after school in the bedroom. [She was] sitting with the light streaming in listening to the shortwave radio. Hitler was speaking in German which my grandmother spoke. She was shouting back in English, "LIAR! LIAR! I got my politics from my grandmother right there in that room.

Thus, Scott Brown learned about injustice first-hand. There and then, her grandmother modeled how a woman can give strong voice including by speaking up against bias. Of course, Jews weren't the only ones experiencing frightening discrimination around that time. In 1948, apartheid was adopted in South Africa, thereby institutionalizing racism and the divide between whites versus "colored"/ blacks. Ironically, given their own family history, her father was "pretty racist." She remembers, "I wasn't brave enough to do anything about apartheid while living in South Africa. I felt I wasn't strong enough. Many people were fighting apartheid. But with my family around me…"[12]

Back then, Scott Brown hadn't yet found her full voice. At twenty, Scott Brown escaped from what must have been the pain and confusion of this political/personal scene, going to London to study at the Architectural Association. Once there, Scott Brown was surprised by the imbalance she encountered in terms of women and architecture. She wondered, "Where are all of the *women* architects?" She'd been surrounded by female designers like her mother all her life. She recalled, "At my university they called the B.A. degree the 'Mrs. Degree.' You didn't go to university to learn something. You went to get married…" Still, her mother had modeled that a women's place need not be just quiet at home.

In fact, when Scott Brown went to England, she left behind not only the South African political/social/cultural backdrop but the man she loved—Robert Scott Brown, the son of an upper-class Scottish father and Jewish mother. Eventually they began to build their lives together. In 1955 when they were both twenty-three, they married and set up house together first in London and then in Philadelphia, where Denise was to obtain a Master's Degree in Architecture and Urban Planning at the University of Pennsylvania.

Hotel lobby representing a traditional Japanese village street, Mielparque Nikko Kirifuri. Hotel and Spa, Nikko, Japan, 1997, designed by Venturi, Scott Brown and Associates, Inc.
Photograph by Kawasumi Architectural Photograph Office. Courtesy Venturi, Scott Brown and Associates, Inc.

Then, suddenly, Robert Scott Brown was killed in a car crash when he was twenty-seven. "I was broken-hearted," she told me. Naturally, during this time of "decisive crisis," Scott Brown was depressed. She felt lost and suffered from a feeling of "structurelessness."[13] After this tragedy, Scott Brown began to teach at University of Pennsylvania's architecture school. Then she went to Berkeley to teach. In the intervening years, she met and married architect Robert Venturi. They settled back in Philadelphia and became partners in the firm of Venturi Scott Brown. The two built their life together. They bought the house where she and I now sat. They had a son.

I fast-forward here because it wasn't her *factual* biography alone that riveted me, it was the *meaning* and *influence* of Denise Scott Brown's woman's journey that I kept digging to reveal. She'd restarted her personal life and launched her professional career, but like Margo Grant Walsh, she still needed to resolve the challenge posed by the bias she had endured and that she witnessed around her.

These South African experiences put her in conflict within herself. She tried to resolve that conflict by leaving home, yet, she reflected:

I did not escape. I felt guilty for leaving and also for living with racism in America. Nor was my marginality, my wanting to be both inside and out, resolved. But at some point I realized it would never be and should not be...Our inner diversity, our conflict about marginality, is both close at hand and deep in our being. Living with it is hard, but it stirs our drives, hones our sensitivities, and makes us unique. It's key to our creativity.[14]

Eventually she confronted her father about his racist attitudes. Looking back, Scott Brown concluded that she did so because she "imbibed rebelliousness from both my mother's early modernism and my African stand against cultural domination."[15]

Besides finding a way to cope with her inner emotional conflict around bias, Scott Brown discovered a design theory that, especially given her personal experiences, clicked for her and led her to devise her own now-famous place-making approach. Sociologist Herbert Gans, one of her University of Pennsylvania professors, raised Scott Brown's consciousness, helping her put her own background in perspective.

In his book, *Popular Culture and High Culture: An Analysis and Evaluation of Taste,*[16] Gans argued that all "taste cultures" are of equal worth. Nevertheless, he believed everyone should have the opportunity to be exposed to a variety of cultures in order to choose the culture they preferred. In Scott Brown's case, Grandmother's tea pot, Mother's modernist white house, and Zoot suits all swirled around her like a multi-cultural kaleidoscope. She recalled:

The African servants we had—you should have seen the way they dressed! I was a very puzzled little girl. They wore rags. I thought they were terribly poor but they wore work rags because they were gardening. Then come Sunday, they'd have Zoot suits on with red buttons on their braces, [suspenders]. That had me really puzzled. What were they?

In truth, when I took Scott Brown through my *Homestyle Exercise* based on Gans's theory, I realized that she was influenced by more "taste cultures" than anyone with whom I'd ever worked: Scott Brown's taste encompassed high, middle, low, and other design cultures that Gans saw as representing a variety of socio-economic groups. All were woven into her multi-culture, environmental story! Gans helped her make sense of such different taste culture combinations. His pluralistic perspective allowed Scott Brown to embrace her own diverse background.

In fact, Scott Brown explained that she'd systematically been analyzing class differences in her head since her youth. She remarked, "I was doing cultural analysis before my time. I had a whole cultural analysis of our school. I didn't know the words like 'elite,' but I [knew] 'popular.' I knew who the girls were who were well-liked, the very popular ones and the ones like me at the other end of the scale."

It's no wonder, then, that she and Venturi created a movement that shifted "high architecture" off its pedestal:

Working at the crossroads of architecture and urbanism, [they] freed architects to embrace history, context, communication, social concern, symbolism, pop art, multi-cultural pluralistic perspectives, and the "messy vitality" of the vernacular. "High art" and "low art" were brought eye-to-eye and purity of expression was challenged by lively impurity."[17]

"Our inner diversity, our conflict about marginality, is both close at hand and deep in our being. Living with it is hard, but it stirs our drives, hones our sensitivities, and makes us unique. It's key to our creativity."
– Denise Scott Brown

Pico Boulevard, Santa Monica, CA, 1966.
Photograph by Denise Scott Brown. Courtesy Venturi, Scott Brown and Associates, Inc.

In fact, that "vitality" of the signs of life in Las Vegas was echoed in her later work such as in the vitality of the design of the Tokyo Hotel Food Court.

Still, Scott Brown herself recognized that her affinity for Las Vegas's neon signs may have come from her own childhood experience of place. She commented:

my grandparents returned from a trip to the New York World's Fair and the tinsel toys brought from Coney Island were beautiful beyond belief to a four-year-old. A second memory is of Johannesburg's 50th Jubilee in the same year. It was my first time out at night and my first neon. They may merely have been commercial street signs, but for me they were a fairyland.[18]

Then, too, given her South African childhood, she pondered, "If the earliest stimuli, the sights and scents experienced when the infant first comes to awareness are in some ways linked to future creativity. ...What are the effects of immigration on the artist?"[19]

Once in America, quite consciously, when it came to reconciling the difference between her grand European-style, Philadelphia home with the nondescript middle-class houses being constructed on her block, Scott Brown reached a place of acceptance in tune with the design-for-diversity she championed. She explained:

I was horrified when I saw what the builder was doing. We made an offer for the site but they wouldn't sell it. Then they subdivided it. I was horrified to see what was happening but then I realized—it really is what I want. 'Nice neighbors who are supportive. ...Look what I have here: an integrated house in an integrated neighborhood.

Having observed a world of cruelty where "insiders" marginalized "outsiders," she very personally understood that physical house and physical neighborhood alone were not substitutes for deep caring and a sense of community. Perhaps Gans's theory provided Scott Brown with a path via which she could heal her own outsider wounds and "return" to consciously embrace an inclusive life/design style. In Design Psychology terms—after her long, winding journey, Scott Brown self-integrated and came fully home.

. . . .

It was getting late that Friday night. Bob Venturi entered the living room to say good-night.[20] He said a gracious good-by to me and exchanged an affectionate fist-bump with his wife, saying, "See you later, alligator." She replied, "See you later, potato." Rather than reflecting a gender stand-off, such a gesture reflected the team spirit in which the couple, their colleagues, and their clients worked together. Scott Brown observed:

Denise Scott Brown with
Arielle Assouline-Lichten
and Caroline James,
Women in Design, Harvard
Graduate School of Design,
2013.
Photographer Unknown

*Bob and I do have our own personalities. ...You see I have ideas all over the place—lots
and lots and lots. Bob has a better ability than me to judge and say, "Okay, let's concen
trate in this way."...He's good at that. I'm good on other ones but you put them together
and it's a good combination. ...The thing that is most helpful is the ping pong of ideas.*

The Yin-Yang nature of their so-successful partnership intrigued me. For Scott
Brown such ping-ponging was a "woman's way of knowing," of sharing ideas:

*Saying that this person, that person helped me—that may be a very feminine outlook,
while a man may say, "All that came out of me (and I do it for you, my darling)." It's
a whole different view of the origin of creativity. And I feel that a woman's view is a
very useful one.* [21]

Given their approach and accomplishments, she certainly possessed the female
qualities of teamwork/cooperation/collaboration as well as high-performance/
quality output. I speculated that her personal experiences of discrimination along
with the tragic death of her first husband helped instill a sense of empathy in her. I
asked Scott Brown if she considered herself a more "thinking" or "feeling" person.
She replied, "Both."

It is testimony to her, then, that she was able to call on both of these aspects of
her "self" to achieve success. Yet, as the sexism described here reveals, such success
didn't come without a fight. Denise Scott Brown's story underscores the tireless
work women have needed to do to make space for themselves and their ways of
knowing and to bring their creative work to the fore. [23]

She thought. She felt. She fought against sexism in architecture. Thus, she
became a model of ways strong women can advocate, can speak out. Scott Brown

pioneered a path for a new generation of designing-women to likewise find their voice. Perhaps most importantly, in *Room at the Top*, she looked back poignantly, writing, "I gain heart and realize that, over the last twenty years, I have managed to do my work and, despite some sliding, to achieve my own self-respect."[22]

If there were a Gold Medal of Place-Making Sociology, I'd award it to Denise Scott Brown, saying: This is a woman who grew up as a marginal person in a wider world of deep divisions and prejudice. She harnessed her vast intelligence, creativity, and sense of empathy to design a more connected, human world. Having won the AIA Gold Medal, she became the most popular girl in architecture town.

**Denise Scott Brown,
Las Vegas Style, 1966.**
Photograph by Robert Venturi

PART II:

Using Lived Experience to Transform Places, Practice, and You

CHAPTER 4:
Transcendent Liberating Design

Driving back to New Jersey that cold, dark night after meeting with Denise Scott Brown, I felt warmed by her heroine's journey. As with each of the designing-women I've discussed, she blazed a trail for other women.

The next day I sat down to contemplate the tales of all of the female place-makers I'd heard. I imagined myself chatting with Julia Morgan, Margaret Grant Walsh and Denise Scott Brown albeit sitting inside in winter without a roaring fire to inspire dialogue (and with spring's birds still so far away). Nevertheless the warp and weft of these women's wise words, my readings, and all our lived experience resulted in my own fabric of beliefs— my answers to the questions I raised at the beginning of this book:

Is there a "woman's way of knowing" crucial to place-making that's been discounted?
I believe:
- *Women in general are culturally conditioned to be more emotional*ly expressive than men.
- Often, women especially have had to mute this "feeling side" and other subjective ways they know in order to succeed in the objectively oriented, traditionally male field of architecture
- As sometimes reflected in space design, hiding one's full persona can create a disjoint between public image and deeper self.

Is there a whole realm of human experience that needs to be laced back into the built world?
I believe:
- Rather than experience a disjoint, we can create places that integrate both our deeper subjective/feeling as well as our objective/thinking sides.
- To create such whole, human-centered places we can use our lived experience as the basis for design.

- Design Psychology's "design from within" process brings such personal environmental experience to the fore so fulfilling design elements can be used to create actualized self/place.

Rather than struggle to fit in, shouldn't women, especially, be pioneering a new way of making environments?
I believe:
- Since women have been given greater cultural "permission" to speak personally about their lives, they are particularly well-positioned to break new ground by using lived experience as the basis for design.
- Thus, as well as using their voices to challenge bias, women can champion human-centercd place-making processes that help overcome oppressions.
- As part of this humanistic wave, the Design Psychology process can be used by anyone to transform places, practice, and one's very sense of self.

Having reached these conclusions, in Part II of this book I want to tell you more about how women and men have turned to using personal experience to shift toward such transformative, what I call "transcendent liberating design" (TLD). Moreover I want to show you how such vital feelings of transcendence and liberation can be released by the Design Psychology process and, ultimately, applied when making place.

. . . .

Transcendent Design

Denise Scott Brown wasn't the first to challenge modernism's tight hold. As early as 1929, Eileen Gray[1], a then famed (yet now, too-little known) designer, declared, "Modern designers have exaggerated the technological side. ...Intimacy is gone, atmosphere is gone. ...Formulas are nothing. ...Life is everything. And life is mind and heart at the same time."[2] Gray's was a clarion call to bring back the human element in place-making. Her warning was so different from that of architectural modernist Adolph Loos who in 1910 famously (now infamously?) linked ornament with crime, declaring Art Nouveau-type ornament (like that on Scott Brown's dresser?) "immoral and degenerate."[3]

Perhaps Gray's call fell on deaf ears: While post-modernism and other architectural isms have come and gone over the years, the pervasive grip of modernism remains strong. As writer/editor Leilah Stone observed in 2020:

Driven by the heroic male architect, Modernist dictates of good design, functionalism, truth to materials, purity of form quickly took over and continue to be the dominant ideology today in the way architecture and interiors are taught and practiced.

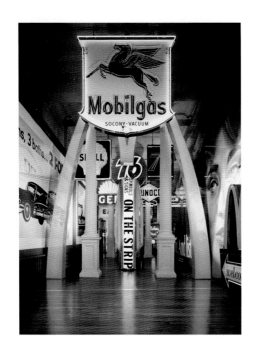

Signs of Life Exhibition, Renwick Gallery, Smithsonian Institute, Washington, DC, 1976.

Photograph by Tom Bernard.

If Modern architecture was rational, masculine, and structural, then decoration was considered emotional, feminine, and shallow.[4]

Renowned architect/theorist Christopher Alexander places blame on our ubiquitous culture. He decries what he sees as society's rational, objective ways of knowing, a way so different from the women's ways of knowing I've been discussing here. Alexander declares:

I believe that we have in us a residue of a world-picture which is essentially mechanical in nature—what we might call the mechanist-rationalist world-picture. ...Like an infection it has entered us, it affects our actions, it affects our moral, it affects our sense of beauty. It controls the way we think when we try to make buildings and—in my view—it has made the making of beautiful buildings all but impossible.[5]

Alternatively, Alexander champions a more subjective, personal—even spiritual approach that aims to create transcendent design. He states, "To reach the ultimate I, the transcendent ground of all existence, you have to reach yourself."[6] Rather than thus calling for a narcissistic "self"-absorption when designing, what Alexander refers to here, is "This self, this 'something' which lies in me and beyond me[7] is nameless, without substance, without form—and yet is also intensely personal"[8] that "is necessary as an underpinning for a successful art of building."[9]

As with Design Psychology, rather than look toward superficial decoration, Alexander's (feminist?) stance turns to deep emotion as luminous, something to be celebrated, not white-washed. In fact, for Alexander, what makes a good place or building is if it seems "alive":[10]

Only a deliberate process of creating being-like (and self-like) centers in buildings throughout the world will encourage the world to become more alive. By this I mean that the successful maker consciously moves towards those things which most deeply reflect or touch his own self, his inner feelings, and consciously moves away from those which do not."[11]

Importantly, although Alexander's emphasis is on places that elicit feeling, he draws a distinction between everyday emotion—happiness, sadness, or anger, for instance, and "emotion" as he defines it: "this feeling as the inward aspect of life.[12] ... in which my vulnerable inner self becomes connected to the world."[13]

Interestingly, too, Joseph Campbell wrote:

The goal of life is rapture
And art is the way we experience it.[14]

I believe that the making of transcendent places can be 'the way we experience' rapture, as well. To achieve such transcendent environments/rapture for ourselves, we can use Design Psychology to "design from within" our very personal lived experience, especially childhood experience of transcendent environments. Long ago, after all, I remember how my elementary school students 'fell in love with the universe' when building their playground and ways my architecture students rediscovered their magical symbiosis with past places while going through Design Psychology's exercises.

Thus it's not modernist design per se to which I object. In fact, I love the design of my own mid-century modern home so reminiscent of my favorite cousins' home of my childhood. My home's simple exterior, angled roof, and huge windows always let in light that uplift me. What Alexander and I critique is modernist buildings devoid of spirit and emotion. For instance, what gripped my own community to construct a high school addition that seems more dead than "alive"? What messages do such structures send to current and future generations about the meaning of architecture—or even the meaning of life?

High School Front (left), High School Rear Auditorium (center), & Gymnasium Addition (right).
Photographs by the author.

Similarly, author Annie Murphy Paul asks, "What thoughts are inspired, what emotions are stirred by a row of beige cubicles, or a classroom housed inside a windowless trailer? This is not simply a question of aesthetics; it is a question of what we think, how we act, who we are."[15]

For example, compare the "dead" gym above right, with the one on next page, built under the direction of Elora Hardy for the Green School in Bali. Rather than follow in modernism's footsteps, that structure "wraps around"[16] students, "holds them, inspires them and nourishes them."[17] It's a space that's alive, transcendent.

Hardy, trained in fine art rather than architecture, is the founder and creative director of "Ibuku," a word that connotes "My Mother Earth" in Balinese. As recommended here, she's brought her personal, environmental, lived experiences to the fore. Consciously or not, she drew from her environmental autobiography when founding Ibuku. Hardy's use of bamboo echoes back to her childhood experience of place growing up in Indonesia.[18] She recalls, "My earliest memory of Bali was my fifth birthday party. I remember making scarecrows together out of thatch,

**Gymnasium, The Arc at Green
School, Bali, designed
by IBUKU.**
Photograph by Tommaso Riva.

**Gymnasium, The Arc at Green
School, Bali, designed
by IBUKU.**
Photograph by Tommaso Riva.

**Sharma Springs
Entrance Tunnel, Bali,
designed by IBUKU.**
Photograph by Rio Helmi.

**Sharma Springs, Bali,
designed by IBUKU.**
Photography by Errol Vaes.

The Oculus World Trade Center Transportation Hub, NYC, designed by Santiago Calatrava.
Shutterstock.

coconut, and bamboo and parading them up to the fields."[19]

In fact, she "designed from within," translating the early imprint of the "babbling rivers, jungle ravines, and artisan-filled villages [that] surrounded her home"[20] in Bali into the transcendent, "deeply spiritual and environmentally friendly plans" she's devised together with her team (as well as consultant Jorg Stamm) for residential, hospitality, and campus spaces.

In 2019, Hardy was named an Honorary Royal Designer for Industry by the Royal Society of Arts, for not only "leading the world in designing buildings from completely renewable resources" but for creating "Buildings that are so naturally beautiful that they promote peace and well-being in everyone that experiences them.[21] Ibuku's buildings engender deep emotional satisfaction. Such transcendent places that mirror the essence of numinous childhood environments inspire us to feel—to deeply *experience* the world, not just to think about or analyze it.

Even in New York City's concrete setting, the Oculus World Trade Center Transportation Hub with its sweeping white wings makes me feel hope within myself. Designed by Santiago Calatrava, its easily recognizable, bird-like form sends an emotional message that we can soar up from 9/11 imagery of smoky, horror-laden scenes. Its symbolism is human-centered, emotion-filled, and relates back to the natural world. The placard near the Oculus explains: "On 9/11 each year, weather permitting, the skylight of the Oculus will be opened to allow the sun to fill this entire space. Envisioned by Santiago Calatrava to symbolize a dove released from a child's hand, the Oculus is situated at an angle in contrast to neighboring buildings and even the entire grid of the city."[22]

. . . .

Have there been other women or men who, like Hardy and Calatrava, have made transcendent places that speak to our emotions and that also, like Scott Brown, bucked the norm to achieve personal as well as "aesthetic liberation?"[23]

To find out, I flew to Scotland. Yes, Scotland! I didn't fly there on a whim. To find precedent, I'd dug back to the turn of the nineteenth century (back to Julia Morgan's, de Wolfe's, and my Great Grandma Rosa's time) and discovered Margaret Macdonald Mackintosh, who studied, worked, and lived in Glasgow during that era. I'd heard of her husband, renowned architect Rennie Mackintosh, but only recently read about Macdonald. In *Having Words*, Denise Scott Brown, likewise, suggests looking carefully at this Scottish couple from a new feminist point of view.[24]

From both a feminist and Design Psychology perspective, their work intrigued me as it often mirrored the "truth," the "transcendental emotion"[25] of what was happening in their lives. Collaboratively, Mackintosh and Macdonald actually designed a variety of places, although Mackintosh alone often is given credit for creating them. Mackintosh famously wrote to his wife, "You must remember that in all my architectural efforts you have been half, if not three-quarters of them."[26] He insisted: "I had talent, but Margaret had genius."[27]

A 1978 exhibition catalog hails the style of the Mackintoshes' jointly designed home as groundbreaking:

> *Together they designed and furnished their first home, an apartment at 120 Mains Street, Glasgow. The drawing room is one of the most important interiors in modern design history. It represents a complete departure from contemporary practice in its whiteness and lightness and freedom from superficial decoration. Every single piece of furniture was designed by the architect in collaboration with his wife, as were the light fittings and other details.*[28]

The Mackintoshes jettisoned the "superficial decoration," of Victorian days and replaced it with a sleek white that heralded the birth of modernism. Yet, importantly, their harbinger-of-modernist style was also "alive" with a sense of emotion, transcendence, and liberation.

Margaret Macdonald, herself, may have led the way since she symbolically expressed soul and spirit[29] in her mediums of watercolor, graphics, textile design, glass, and some metalwork. Rather than depict saccharine images of ideal sweet, coy women[30] of the Victorian era, Macdonald's mystery paintings, for instance, illustrated the more authentic roles that women played while on their women's journey: "wife, mother, mourner, sexual woman, celibate woman, and celebrant."[31]

In terms of creating a sense of transcendence in places, although originally influenced by the Arts and Crafts movement, both Macdonald and Mackintosh eventually became associated with the symbolist movement, which illuminated "the soul that lies beneath."[32] In fact, Mackintosh "spoke of transmitting 'instinct,' 'emotion,' and 'poetry' through his work, all of which were identified with the more spiritual female persona."[33]

Perhaps the first wave of feminism that swept through during the early 1900s influenced the couple's more emancipatory style or perhaps their style mirrored their own relationship which was one of equals. The push for women's rights during their era also may have made it easier to have not just an egalitarian marriage, but to create egalitarian space which reflected this new kind of relationship between women and men. In their white rooms, as one critic has observed: The "feminine" that is remade is not domestic, but innovatory and fantastic...[it's] neither persecutory nor subservient....one in which the attainment of modernity is dependent on a change in the relations between the sexes in which the "feminine" is the site

Margaret Macdonald Mackintosh.
Courtesy The Glasgow School of Art.

The Mysterious Garden by Margaret Macdonald Mackintosh.
National Galleries of Scotland. Scottish National Gallery of Modern Art, Edinburgh: Purchased with the help of the Art Fund 2011.

The White Dining Room (Ladies Luncheon Room), Miss Cranston's Ingram Street Tearoom, Glasgow, 1900 attributed to C.R. Mackintosh with The May Queen panel by Margaret Macdonald.
© CSG CIC Glasgow Museums Collection.

of innovation.[34] Overall such "fashioning of the new interior was, by analogy, a refashioning of the inner life to meet the demands of a new age."[35]

What did their spaces actually look like? As with Scott Brown and Venturi, the Mackintoshes embraced the use of symbolism that was immediately recognizable to all. Yet, unlike those post-modernists, Macdonald/ Mackintosh's symbolism was deliberately chosen because it was highly personal[36] and carried emotion and soul.[37] It seems no wonder, then, that I was drawn to their work which seemed almost "religious in achieved quality."[38] For the Mackintoshes, the rose, for instance, a traditional feminine motif with its quintessential sensual and spiritual beauty, perfectly represented "life's potentiality." Although a well-used, universal symbol from time immemorial, the Mackintoshes embraced it as their own.[39]

Here as well, however, one glance at interiors or furniture incorporating the "Glasgow Rose" and the name

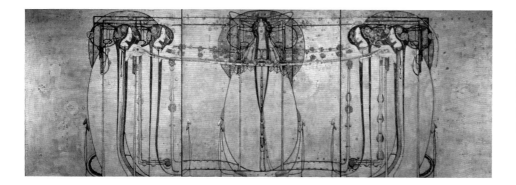

The May Queen wall panel by Margaret Macdonald Mackintosh, 1900. Original location: Ladies Luncheon Room, Miss Cranston's tea rooms, Ingram St., Glasgow.
Wikipedia Commons

"Mackintosh," not Macdonald, pops to mind. Yet his-tory is often a her-story, too. The original inspiration for the Mackintosh rose may have come from the so long-disparaged "women's work" (like that of Great Grandma Rosa's sewing circle!). Female textile designer, Jessie Newberry, in particular, played a major role in shaping what became known as the Glasgow Style.[40] Newberry first designed and embroidered the rose shown right,[41] that now seems so similar to the rose of the Scottish Art Nouveau style the Mackintoshes ushered in (below right). Regardless, Macdonald and Mackintosh together collaborated on the design of interiors like those for Miss Cranston's tea rooms, which became some of the most well-known examples of the Mackintoshes' widely admired projects. Macdonald's gesso pieces or long friezes often were incorporated in such interiors that overall were "sumptuous" but "serene," suggesting "intimacy and sensuality."[42]

Cushion cover embroidery by Jessie Newberry, circa 1900.
@ CSG CIC Glasgow Museums and Libraries Collections.

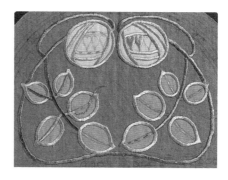

Their work gained more acclaim in Europe than in the UK. At one point, the Mackintoshes, flowers at their feet, were carried through the streets in Vienna. By the early 1900s, however, Art Deco's simple forms and sense of luxury replaced emotional expression. Modernism's dictum "form follows functions" signaled not only the death of ornament, but also the use of symbolism to evoke emotions.[43] Gradually the Mackintoshes slipped into near obscurity. The approach of World War I with its increasing nationalism and chauvinism meant the subjectivity of individual expression fell out of favor and limited opportunities for the couple.[44] In reduced circumstances, C. R. Mackintosh died in 1928, Margaret in 1933. Thus the Mackintoshes ushered in a new expressive, modern style yet it morphed into a modernism devoid of emotions that contributed to their own professional demise.

Rose and Teardrop textile design by C.R. Mackintosh, 1916-23.
© The Hunterian, University of Glasgow.

Still, they left behind for us a model of transcendent, liberating design as reflected in their white apartment space, now part of the Hunterian Art Gallery in Glasgow,[45] that I promptly went to see. Although all white, it's filled with expression. I could describe the house to you room by room but I don't want to spoil your experience. (Words alone can't describe it anyway. You have to visit it.) Nevertheless, once I entered the Macdonald/Mackintosh bedroom, I understood why their house was called "an oasis, a revelation, a delight." [46]

I sense that you are curious. Okay, I invite you to walk into their bedroom. Imagine you are Eve or Adam (or "they"—not "she" or "he") entering an all-ivory-colored Garden of Eden for the first time—a simple sensual, sculptural space with swirling white leaf-forms and (here and there) pops of red and blue and green inlay.

Lie down on the simple, white four-poster bed. Imagine all is quiet and still. Ephemeral, the drapes are parted, window open so wind can reach the fireplace nearby you, keeping the fire alive. Look out and watch the sun or moon rise; the sun or moon set. The sun or moon rise. The sun or moon set. Is there a lover, muse, or soulmate you want to join you there? Close your eyes and go deep into the heart of things. . .Open your eyes and rise. Look into the room's full-length mirror and notice that you are naked to your fully revealed self.

What do you think? What do you feel? Do *you* want to create Transcendent Liberating Design?

Liberating Design

How, then, can we capture the intimacy of our *emotional* story of place yet, at the same time achieve a sense of liberation, too? Are there other modern-day Macdonald/Mackintoshes making transcendent liberating place? After all, the modernism and then minimalism that left this Scottish couple behind also left "no place for identity, history, race, gender, the personal, the private. Period."[1]

Thankfully (although not eliminating modernism's hold) at least Scott Brown and Venturi shook things up. Championing diverse cultural narrative, they invited us to view McDonald's arch as a portal to pass through from strictly modernist, all-white space to a more inclusive world.

Increasingly, in fact, during the feminist third and fourth waves, many others have been exploring and expressing their personal, as well as intersectional identities via place-making. In design education, too, new, more inclusive ways of learning are evolving. For example, North Carolina State University assistant professor Lesley-Ann Noel has created a nine-point manifesto "towards changing the conversation around race, equity, and bias in design."[2] Citing Paulo Freire as a major influence, the first point she makes in her manifesto is, "Start everything with positionality!"[3]

What does Noel mean by "positionality"? Who was Friere? In his classic book, *Pedagogy of the Oppressed*[4], published in 1970, renowned Brazilian educator Friere laid out a revolutionary method of using lived experience as the basis for adult education that still remains influential. It's a book my old "education-as-factory" principal would have hated! In it, Freire railed against the "banking" model of education wherein teachers deposit knowledge. He argued that such a mode of education turns students into "receiving objects. ...attempts to control thinking and action, leads men and women to adjust to the world, and inhibits their creative power."[5]

Instead, through a process of consciousness-raising, what Friere called "conscientization"[6] people become aware of themselves as "positioned" in their life circumstance: They *"develop their power to perceive critically the way they exist in the world with which and in which they find themselves; they come to see the world not as a static reality but as a reality in the process of transformation."*[7]

Through Freire's method, illiterate students, victims of poverty, became aware of the ocean of oppression that engulfed them. Thus the students gained insight about their social/cultural context and how they, themselves, could change their circumstances. More conscious and motivated, many students learned to read in forty-five days.

Thus, overall, Freire's work focused not only on literacy as traditionally defined, but on an empowering kind of "self-literacy" obtained via critical understanding of one's own lived experience. No doubt Friere's consciousness-raising call is one the authors of *Women's Ways of Knowing* would have loved! Similarly, the Design Psychology process aims to raise people's awareness of their lived social and emotional experience so they can give voice to it via the creation of transcendent liberating design.

When it comes to liberating design, in fact, there are individuals and groups worldwide that are claiming their voices via the creation of actual and even virtual place. Well-aware of historical inequalities when it comes to architecture and design, the Black Arts + Designers Guild (BADG), for example, aims to shift the culture since their goal is "to dismantle those inequities for our members, present and future by creating opportunities and raising awareness."[8] Speaking with a clear, strong voice, BADG's manifesto declares[9]:

- We are **LIBERATORY** - committed to defining new social constructs and rejecting all forms of oppression.
- We are **CELEBRATORY** - embracing Black creative joy in all its glorious manifestations.
- We are **COLLABORATIVE** - sharing knowledge, resources, labor, and insight to bring new diasporic creativity into the world.
- We are **COMMUNITY** - knowing that we thrive more wholly in solidarity than alone.
- We are **ACTIVE** - embodying the spirit of making over all else.
- We are **ACTIVISTS** - showing up, speaking up, and demanding equity through and for our work.
- We **BELIEVE** in ourselves and in the possibilities we can bring to life through art and design.

In 2020, with this manifesto as a touchstone, twenty-three members of (BADG)[10] who work in the arts, architecture, and interior design, collaborated to imagine a virtual house[11] to be experienced on the internet. The resulting "Obsidian Virtual Concept House," is a "futurist dwelling" that "embraces possibility and freedom for a Black family through design"[12] (see: https://obsidianbybadg.house/).

Apropos of human-centered place, BADG founder Malene Barnett, declared that the home is a container for feeling not just a physical space.[13] Yet it also "is a supporting space for the mental, physical, and spiritual well-being of the Black family and all of its expressions of joy and creativity."[14]

Apropos of environmental autobiography, the interiors of the house are "all informed by the creators' unique family histories and approaches to design."[15] Barnett declares, "By returning home to the legacy of the past, we can move forward." The Concept Home's "Sankofa-Legacy Wall," for instance, is composed of ceramic tiles inscribed with ancestral names.[16] She explains: "Within the tradition with African symbolism, the wall evokes Sankofa, the Adinkra concept meaning, 'go back and get it.' This is a necessary mindset to reclaim our Black identity and greatness. These walls send daily affirmations of self-love and inspire ways to be an active member of the community. ...The wall is a metaphor for 'our ingenuity, strength, and perseverance.'" [17]

Barnett, herself, translates such messages into real, not just virtual, works of art and design. Interestingly, in terms of environmental autobiography, she states, "I use pattern and color to transform any surface using marks and motifs that evoke memories from the past. It was early childhood trips to the Caribbean, then extensive travels through Africa, Southeast Asia, and Europe that gave me reverence for the repetition of color and patterns."[18]

With this in mind, I glance at the "Blend" rug that she designed. At first it seems to show a series of abstract shapes. (Perhaps that's all she intended.) Yet studying it as an almost Rorschach-like image, I see exuberant women dancing free. Such work seems transcendent, liberating, and inspiring to me. Like Margaret Macdonald Mackintosh, she's created imagery that is personal, evocative, and emancipatory.

When it comes to such empowerment, you might think design + transcendence + women's liberation make strange "bed*females*." Yet now I am going to tell you the story of a female icon of the women's liberation movement who, much to my surprise, used the psychology of design to raise her own, individual awareness and to help overcome oppression that she, herself, had internalized.

"Blend," hand-knotted wool/ silk rug by Malene Barnett.
Bequia Wallpaper, Kindred Collection, Marlene Barnett for Lulu + Georgia.

Gloria Steinem.
Shutterstock.

Gloria Steinem

Gloria Steinem doesn't have the professional place-maker letters AIA, FAIA, ASID, or IIDA[1] after her name. Instead, "heroine" might be the title that best covers the breadth of her career/resume: spokeswoman for the women's movement in the late 1960s and early 1970s, co-founder of *Ms. Magazine*, political activist, feminine organizer, lecturer, and writer. To my surprise, she also harnessed the psychological power of place to design her home "from within" to help love herself.

In her book *Revolution from Within: A Book of Self-Esteem*,[2] Steinem speaks from her experience when she cautions women "about the dangers of achieving success without doing the necessary groundwork for self-love and self-esteem."[3] She recounts how, despite her success, she, too, lacked a sense of self-worth. Apropos of "Internalized Oppression," Steinem declared, "The truth was that I had internalized society's *unserious* estimate of all that was female—including myself."[4] She suffered from her own "wound of the feminine."

Through therapy, she too began to unpack her environmental autobiography and gain insight about ways her itinerant childhood had impacted her. Writing about "Coming Home" she states:

> Only after fifty did I begin to admit that I was suffering from my own form of imbalance. Though I felt sorry for myself for not having a home, I was always rescued by defiance and a love of freedom. ...Like [my father], I'd saved no money, so there was a good reason for my fantasy of ending up as a bag lady. I handled it just by saying to myself, I'll organize the other bag ladies.

> Finally, I had to admit that I too was leading an out-of-balance life, even if it was different in degree from my father's. I needed to make a home for myself; otherwise it would do me in, too. Home is a symbol of the self. Caring for a home is caring for one's self.[5]

"The home as symbol of self"! Had she read Clare Cooper Marcus's article, "The House as Symbol of Self,"[6] which so long ago convinced me of the intertwining of sense of self and home? Regardless, when reading *Revolution from Within*, I was intrigued that Steinem sometimes used "place" terms to describe how she turned to therapy to break down the "brick wall" she'd built between herself and her childhood.[7] She'd "walled" herself off from emotion and lost her "voice."[8]

To help her gain insight and recapture her sense of self, Steinem's therapist, Nancy Napier,[9] took her through past-*place* guided meditations She suggested to Steinem, "Close your eyes and remember yourself as a little girl in 'a safe place that is beautiful and private.'"[10] Steinem traveled deep into her unconscious, recalling scenes from her environmental autobiography:

There I am in a small room with white walls dappled in summer sunlight. It is hot. There is a little girl of five or six, wearing a worn out red bathing suit, lying on the cool sheets of a bed where she feels relaxed and poured out like molasses. I know she's been outside all day catching turtles that she keeps in a tub in the backyard, then lets go again at summer's end. ...The sight of that bed also brings back the sensations of nights too hot to sleep and the cooling drift of talcum powder on my skin. It also brings an image of being awakened by my father for a midnight swim, then tip toeing downstairs, feeling grown-up because things look strange in the moonlight and my father wants my company.

Mostly as this little girl, I feel filled with the pleasure of good tiredness, going barefoot; feeling unself-conscious and being at home in my body. The words Wild Child come into my mind and make me smile. [11]

Steinem then recognized that there were other transcendent, outdoor spaces like the ocean that made her feel connected to the universe. She explains, "standing at the edge of this mysterious three fourths of the planet from which we all evolved, we feel returned to some authentic, calming, inner core of ourselves, as if the mere sight of it could wash away all artifice and confusion."[12] The opposite of the lonely landscapes of her childhood, such environments gave her comfort.[13] Over time, such therapeutic visualization helped Steinem retrieve her "wild child," her emotional, inner core as well as a sense of wholeness.

Similarly, as part of the Design Psychology process, I take people through my *Favorite Place Visualization Exercise.* I read a script that allows them to free-float to a favorite *past*-place in their mind's eye:

Relax. Listen to your breathing. Close your eyes. Make sure you are comfortable. Breathe easily...Begin to remember another favorite place—perhaps a place you haven't thought about in a long time. Some favorite place from childhood, a country or city place, an inside or outside place...

My script continues with carefully chosen words that elicit images, sensory memories, and emotions of past places—often long-forgotten chapters of one's environmental story. Once participants open their eyes, they frequently report that the visualization transported them emotionally to a different time and transcendent place.[14] Just like those kids (wild children?) I taught so long ago who loved digging in the earth to build their tire playground, these adults dug deeply *within* to remember when they too were "in love with the universe."[15]

Design Psychology was never meant to be any kind of therapy. Steinem's therapist, however, incorporates past place memories as part of the traditional, long-effective art therapy technique of having patients draw pictures of their emotional experiences. Thus, Steinem observes:

I've painted or drawn what I saw; for instance, the basement room where a scared eleven-year-old lies on the top of a bunk bed while her mother sleeps beneath. Though stick figures are all I can manage, I find it's the colors that count. Grey is for the ceiling that the little girl stares at to pretend nothing else exists, dark brown is for the horizontal figures of her and her mother lying on their narrow beds—and purple is for the healing witness of my future self who is entering the doorway. [16]

To help Steinem color her world differently, Napier tapped into positive, rather than such negative environmental imagery. She suggested that Steinem visualize herself in a natural setting walking on a path in a forest, meadow, seashore, or mountains that felt beautiful and safe. Her therapist prompted her to imagine that place in all its sensory detail. Steinem writes:

I began to see a forest of pine trees with a path that seemed to parallel an ocean, yet also drew closer so that, in the distance through the trees, the ocean itself was visible. As usual, my visual sense was strongest, but I had intimations of the crunch of pine needles beneath my feet, the tang of salt and pine in the air, and the feel of dappled sunlight under trees...

This path was a part of my life's journey...My conscious self was an observer, a passenger, and my deeper self was the voyager. Ahead of me on the path was someone walking where I had yet to travel. It was my future self, the person I wanted to become, an optimal self who was leading me. [17]

Ms. Magazine 1972 "Wonder Woman for President" cover. Reprinted by permission of *Ms. Magazine,* © 1972.

Eventually, through such drawing and place visualizations, Steinem realized that she could connect both with her creative "child-self" as well as "the strength and wisdom of her future self." [18] Moreover, rather than just *envision* her future best self, she surmised that she could translate her vision and, as part of her personal transformation, create a healthy, fulfilling *place.*

With this in mind, she knew that her adult New York City apartment was an unconscious, unhealthy repetition of her childhood home, rather than a re-creation of any positive, even transcendent, place experiences. She explains, "I remembered longing to escape the littered, depressing, rat-infested house where I lived alone with my mother; yet I had recreated an upscale, less dramatic version of it in my own apartment with cardboard boxes, stacks of papers, and long absences." [19] Instead of continuing to repeat this pattern, Steinem felt the time had come to make a home for herself.[20] Thus she asked friends to help her move the stacks of cardboard boxes, so that the apartment would not just be livable, but also *pleasant*.[21] She writes about the transformation:

> *Gradually, the rooms that I had used mostly as an office and a closet were filled with things that gave me pleasure when I opened the door. I had a kitchen that worked, a real desk to spread papers on, and a welcoming room where visiting friends could stay, something I'd always wanted as a child when I was living with my mother in places too sad to invite anyone.*[22]

"Nesting," as she purchased things like sheets and candles, Steinem finally jettisoned the "melancholy feeling." She'd internalized that "Everybody has a home but me."[23] Continuing to expand figuratively and literally, over the years, she purchased not just her two-story walk-up apartment, but also the entire three-story New York City brownstone. Then, upon reaching her eighties, Steinem established Gloria's Foundation to support and nurture the feminist movement she'd championed for so long. The Foundation's first goal was to take ownership of some and, ultimately, all of Steinem's brownstone. The idea was for it to continue to be used as "a center for activism, thought, creativity, security, and planning."[24]

In 2021, in fact, to mark Steinem's eighty-seventh birthday, "A Home for a Movement,"[25] a virtual exhibit of her home, went digitally on display. (See: https:// artsandculture.google.com/story/a-home-for-a-movement/jgIi1197UxiDIA) I visited the apartment (virtually, that is). There for all to see are her mementos of international travels, her collection of elephants and turtles, and other special objects. (Are those turtles really totems, reminding her of those summers she visualized – positive memories of her wild child relaxing in her backyard?)

Not being there in person, I virtually eyed instead the framed first issue of *Ms. Magazine* showing "Wonder Woman as President" and posters of famous activists who've led the struggle to set women free. Then, too, the exhibit literally has captured the voices of other feminist movement heroines. Its virtual gallery includes voice recordings of Bella Abzug, Dorothy Pitman Hughes,[26] and other inspiring feminist leaders whose rousing words moved the Women's Liberation Movement forward.

Looking back, Steinem wished that her mother and other women could have moved forward on the paths they loved.[27] Perhaps that's why Steinem's home will be left "just so" as a political meeting space where, in the future, women can meet and feel safe."[28] Steinem comments, "My mother did not have to give up a journey of her own to have a home." Steinem reassures us, "Neither do I. Neither do you."[29]

Interestingly she concludes, "If we ever have a second chance at the past, it is the unconscious that gives it to us. We can go home again because a part of us never left."[30] Stories such as Steinem's point to how, consciously, we can create fulfilling spaces that support our positive change and growth. In my case, as I'll tell you next, it was a challenge to my physical, not mental, well-being that stopped me in my tracks and made me not only take place "design therapy" seriously but actually use it to heal myself.

"If we ever have a second chance at the past, it is the unconscious that gives it to us. We can go home again because a part of us never left."–Gloria Steinem

CHAPTER 5:
Healing by Design Psychology

The Road to Wellness[1]

One day, after being back in America for many years, I received a call from a reporter doing a story about an artist redesigning her home as a catalyst for her recovery from breast cancer. The reporter asked my opinion. I commented, "Researchers are just beginning to understand the connection between physical health, psychology, and home."[2] Two weeks later, I was diagnosed with early stage breast cancer.

Healing bedroom oasis created by the author via Design Psychology.
Photograph by the author.

Faced with a good prognosis, but with the reality of this diagnosis, I wondered if there was a way to use Design Psychology as part of my own therapeutic process. I'd always used Design Psychology to look to the *past* for place-making inspiration. Now, however, what I wanted to do was live—to have a *future*. I decided to envision myself on the road to that *healthy* future, as Gloria Steinem had done. I imagined my healing journey and embarked on the real-life redesign of my home, albeit of my bedroom. My transformation of that space became a catalyst for and symbol of my own self-transformation from sickness to health.

Steinem remembered her childhood world as colored with depressing gray and dark brown. Today her yellow walls are uplifting. How did I first color my space to send healing, not demoralizing, messages to my psyche? Since my bedroom is at the end of a long hallway, I began by painting the room's back wall a deep, dark blue. I painted the other three walls of the bedroom a full-of-life springtime green. From the far end of the hallway, each time I returned from my daily radiation sessions, it looked as if I were walking down the hall toward a blue, depressing space. Yet once I'd reached the bedroom's threshold, the green walls opened to light and hope. This use of color acted as a trigger, a metaphor reminding me "there's light at the end of the tunnel."

Next, warned that radiation treatment often produced fatigue and radiation burn, I purchased "cucumber cool" cotton sheets and luxury bedding that would help me imagine being cooled down. A shimmering bed throw and the ocean blue and light green wall colors aided my "cool" visualization.

I then added design elements to help me visualize my longed-for-future. I surrounded myself with fabrics, furniture, window treatments, floor coverings, and special objects that reminded me of my long-held desire to learn to sail. On one side of my bed, for instance, I placed a painting of a sailboat in a storm surrounded by rocks symbolizing where I'd been. On the other side of the bed I hung a painting of a sailboat moored safely at sunset—where I wanted to go. I also hung new curtains from subtle porthole-like openings. Beige Berber carpet evoked a sandy beach underfoot. Think, subtle. Absent were any tacky "Ahoy Matey" signs or captain's wheel.

The author in her bedroom wearing the prototype for the 'Robe to Wellness'. Photograph by the author.

Meanwhile, I also wore a golden embroidered Chinese robe to each treatment rather than the usual bland hospital gown. Wearing that dramatic garb, during radiation sessions I took myself through a guided visualization imagining myself an empress on a healing journey, staring down cancer.

The result? Much to my doctor's surprise, I suffered none of the usual radiation burn. I have no objective, scientific data to prove that my Design Psychology intervention was the miracle ingredient that prevented it. I do know that my bedroom project definitely gave me a *feeling* of control when things felt out of control. I began the project on my first day of treatment and finished on my last day. A week later—given the all-clear and a prognosis of an extremely low chance of recurrence—I was off to Florida to learn to sail.

So glad to be alive, I vowed to expand my Design Psychology methodology to help others shift their focus from their past or scary present to envisioning positive future dreams. I experimented with ways Design Psychology as place therapy might help other women achieve both physical and mental health.

Throughout my cancer treatment, for example, I regularly stopped by the Princeton Y.W.C.A. Breast Cancer Resource Center (BCRC), a place that "supports improving access to women's health and empowering women to take control over their physical, mental, and emotional well-being."[3] For forty-one years, the BCRC had been operating free support groups, wellness programs, and a prosthesis and wig bank out of their cramped warren of meeting, counseling, and office rooms.

Knowing from my own lived experience about the importance of a nurturing, healing place, I conducted a *Healing Oasis by Design*[4] workshop at the Center. The goal of the three-session workshop series was to devise a plan for BCRC's transformed space. Knowing from Freire about the importance of involving people in their own transformation, I also aimed to involve patients and staff in BCRC's renovation as part of a therapeutic process. Then, too, I wanted to experiment with ways women could collaborate and uniquely use their collective lived experience to make a place for a group, not just for themselves, individually.

With all of this in mind, I adapted Design Psychology's exercises so that workshop participants could open their treasure chests of favorite past *healing* places. The *Guided Visualization Exercise*, for instance, helped them recall design elements—colors, textures, furniture, and special objects—that had primal, nurturing associations for them.[5]

> *Close your eyes and imagine arriving at a beautiful oasis—perhaps a favorite, nurturing place from your past where you went to relax and renew yourself.*

The *Toolbox's* visualization exercise retrieved transcendent memories of such past healing oases. Using the information gleaned from these exercises, participants completed the *Ideal Place Exercise* by combining their oasis memories and associations to form one statement for BCRC's ideal new space:

> *Our ideal BCRC space is a warm and welcoming oasis providing balance, calm, and empowerment. It is a personal, nurturing, homey place where we bring strength to each other and allow women to reach their full potential. The use of water, plants, sunshine, and other natural materials in the space reflects BCRC's place as a touchstone for hope, healing, and community where women can feel unstoppable.*

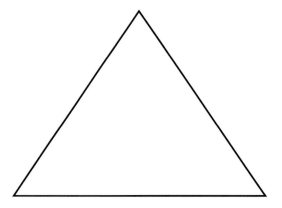

Although the primary emphasis here was on the *Center's* renovation, each group member also did simultaneously envision a *home* retreat for themselves. Each participant came up with her own, unique ideal oasis vision to help her imagine a positive, healthy *future* as expressed in a transcendent, liberating space. When it came to a sense of liberation, for example, by completing my *Place Sociogram Exercise*,[6] these women gained insight about the importance of establishing healthy boundaries.

As a result, each woman then devised a plan for a home bedroom, meditation area, reading nook, or other private space for peace, quiet, and healing—what one might call their "She-Space." When it came to the Design Psychology Blueprint developed for the Center's *group* space, recommendations included reconfiguring it to establish a separate waiting area, meeting space, wig/prosthesis fitting area, and storage space there.

Once the BCRC blueprint was finalized, faster than I could say "Gloria Steinem," BCRC's education director[7] took charge and measured their space, created a floor plan, selected furniture, flooring, and paint based on their oasis by design vision. White furniture and a bold blue/green (not pink) color scheme, for instance, were all part of the plan to provide a transcendent, life-enhancing aura there.

Overall, as with any expressive arts therapy, the point wasn't to create designing-women "Professionals" with a capital 'P', or to ignore the important role played by designers. Involving non-professionals in this participatory design process imbued them with the power that results from the art of place-making. Then, too, it helped debunk the myth that only designers have a reservoir of design tales to tell. Shortly thereafter, BCRC's director[8] relocated to the West Coast, but commented, "I see BCRC's transformation as part of my legacy."

Fortunately, in these intervening years, a wave of interest in healthcare design has inspired new projects and programs resulting in an amazing array of soothing healthcare settings.[9] I worked on just a few[10] but then developed one more healing

BEFORE version of Princeton YWCA Breast Cancer Resource Center.
Photograph by the author.

AFTER version of Princeton YWCA Breast Cancer Resource Center.
Photograph by the author.

The "Robe to Wellness" radiation/hospital gown.
Photograph by the author.

project to help other women battling breast cancer visualize their empowered selves. Remembering the Chinese robe I'd worn to my radiation treatment, I used it as a prototype for a *Robe to Wellness* radiation gown for other women. First, relying on data suggesting that views of nature heal,[11] I chose a eucalyptus-leaf pattern for the robe's silky fabric that fit with its kimono style.

Next I invited anyone around the world to post a "Well-Wishes" message on www.robetowellness.com. In a weekly Robe to Wellness Sewing Circle, patients, survivors, and other volunteers then stitched such messages as, "In deep waters, friends carry you," or "You are gently held in love and care," on to each gown's collar. Thus, drawing on their "ethic of care," women supported women in sewing circles. As in Great Grandma Rosa's time, the gathered group told their stories, laughed, and swapped recipes as they stitched. Now, each Robe to Wellness is a walking work of art in hospitals worn by "royal" women moving along their healing path.

Overall, then, while on my road to wellness, I thought these projects were just a detour on my North Star quest to use psychology and design to nurture a fulfilling sense of self. Instead, my journey led me to discover ways psychology can help heal by design.

The "Neuros," Women, and Metaphoria

In fact, when I step back and think about psychology's contribution to making a healing place, I know that the ever-expanding field of *neuroscience* has become a touchstone in the world of healthcare spaces in particular. The focus of neuroscience in architecture is on the objective, biological workings of the nervous system and brain, rather than on creating places based on subjective lived experience. So important is this new data-driven direction, the Academy for Neuroscience in Architecture coalesced in 2002. It's declared:

> *Some observers have characterized what is happening in neuroscience as the most exciting frontier of human knowledge since the Renaissance. All humanity stands to benefit from this research in countless ways still to be determined. The profession of architecture has become a partner in developing the application of this knowledge base.[1]*

While therapists like mine and Gloria Steinem's use psychology to help us understand our invisible, emotional foundations, neuropsychologists use their scientific tools to examine the more observable building block of our lives. Neuro*psychology* (a branch of neuroscience), for instance, examines the relationship between the brain, behavior, and emotion.

When applied to design, Neuroscience/Neuropsychology informs and guides. For example, findings in these neuro fields may explain why my bedroom design worked so well: one study suggests that "people feel cooler in cool-toned rooms and warmer in warm-toned rooms, although actual temperature may be the same."[2] *Perhaps* that's why, thanks to my cool colors, I got no radiation burn.

Another study explains that "people who have learned to associate a place with a positive feeling—or with hopes that the place will heal—will benefit from simply being in that place."[3] Maybe the association I made between my new bedroom décor and a sailing future helped me remain positive throughout my treatment. Mostly I think that just the *process* of redesigning my space calmed me down, since science shows that a trick of reducing the stress response is to fool your brain into thinking you have some degree of control.[4]

Then, too, when it comes to my Design Psychology tools, such scientific findings help explain why the most powerful exercise I use to uncover people's childhood attachment to oases is my *Favorite Place Visualization Exercise* like the one Steinem's therapist used. Pointing to the scientific workings of the mind, guided visualization expert, Bellaruth Naparstek (a social worker, not a neuroscientist) suggests that such guided visualization "sidesteps the logical, analytical part of our brains,"[5] the more "literal" aspects of our minds. Thus, according to her, images send their, "healing messages straight into the center of the whole person,"[6] where they are "floating soft, appealing reminders of health, strength, meaning, and hope."[7]

Convinced of the power of science to so inform, healthcare architects and interior designers have embraced a whole movement called "evidence-based design" (EBD)—design guided by research findings and "verifiable proof."[8] Yet even Kirk Hamilton, an evidence-based hospital design research expert, observes, "not all or even most decisions will be ideally evidence based. ...Good projects...contain the magic of the human spirit, infused with the sacred, the grand, the intimate, and full richness of Life."[9]

Similarly, when it comes to "scientizing"[10] design, there actually may be a feminist issue here too. As interior design educator Jill Pable points out, subjectivity (and the interior design profession as a whole) historically has been undervalued due to negative association between "the feminine" and the emotional—a subjective sensibility so different from a data-driven way to know.[11] With this in mind, Pable sees the need for a "Renewed Balance in Subjective and Objective Ways of Knowing."[12] She looks to a more "integrated age" of "personalization, collaboration, and a reconciled comfort with intuitive and subjective modes of knowing and acting."[13]

Similarly, design educator/theorist Lucinda Kaukas Havenhand, sees interior design, particularly, as a field that can acknowledge "the person first" and put emotions and empathy at the forefront.[14] As she sees it, these characteristics, "reside in and are identified as feminine,"[15] yet they have been marginalized.

Still, it's thanks to neurobiology that we've confirmed that the "right-brained" qualities of "imagination," "expression," and "emotional intelligence," often considered the domain of females, are more a product of socialization than biology. Our analytical and methodological "left brain" also isn't inherently "male," as oft purported. In fact, neuroscience shows that, rather than operating separately,[16] both sides of all of our brains actually have an *inter*dependent working relationship. All the more reason why all of us can draw from both hemispheres to create a more human, balanced built world. But how?

Finnish architect and thinker Juhani Pallasmaa's suggests we design based on both our "lived" as well as analytic experience including via the use of metaphoric imagery to express our very existence:

the designer and the artist need existential knowledge moulded by their experiences of life. Existential knowledge arises from the way the person experiences and expresses his/her existence. ...In design work, these two categories of knowledge [science and art] merge, and as a consequence, the building is a rational object of utility and an artistic/existential metaphor at the same time.[17]

Of course, the idea of using metaphor isn't something new to place makers. Just one glance at the sail-like form of Sydney's iconic Opera House and the grandeur of its harbor floats across our minds.

Yet as you saw with my sailing bedroom, I champion the use of metaphoric design elements that move one forward on the journey of self-evolution. Thus, now I embrace "metaphoria"—love of metaphor—as another tool to use when creating transcendent, liberating design. In fact, I've come across two books with metaphoria in their titles by authors similarly enraptured by metaphor + people + place.

In their book *Marketing Metaphoria*,[18] Harvard professor emeritus Gerald and Lindsay Zaltman turn to neuroscience to explain metaphors' power. The Zaltmans suggest that *both deep metaphors and emotions* are "siblings. ...hard-wired in our brains" although shaped by our social environments and experiences as well.[19] They posit that (before we even speak) metaphors play "powerfully, yet silently"[20] within us.

Interestingly, then, via their consumer research, the Zaltmans identified seven "giant" metaphors including, "transformation" and "journey."[21] Just as I fixed on sailing elements when decorating to symbolize my past, present, and future life-journey, so the Zaltmans similarly observe:

Journey is one of the most widely examined and universally felt deep metaphors and appears as a major theme in literature around the world. Journey is rooted in our awareness of time, evolution, progress, and maturation.[22]*...Our sense of the past, present, and future often combine to create the experience of a physical, social, or psychological journey.*[23]

Accordingly, they developed and applied a Zaltman Metaphor Elicitation Technique (ZMET)[24] to excavate and use such giant metaphors to help design *places*. For example, the architecture firm Astorino used the ZMET technique to explore the minds of future users of a $500 million state-of-the-art facility for the Children's Hospital of Pittsburgh that Astorino was designing. The study determined that *transformation* was the giant metaphor intrinsic to hospital user experience. Such transformation included not only physical transformation (i.e., patients changing from sick to healed), but emotional transformations (e.g., from an anxious to a calm state after a successful surgery).[25]

Astorino then translated the deep metaphor of transformation into design elements. For instance, the team used butterflies, "an archetypical expression of transformation,"[26] in hospital corridors and entrances. Likewise, around the hospital they displayed both artwork expressing transformation and poems with transformational language gleaned from interviews. Such metaphoric messages were intended to positively distract yet also reach people emotionally by helping to soothe and engender optimism.[27]

In the other book entitled *Metaphoria*,[28] author Rubio Battino also utilizes the metaphors of journey and transformation. Yet, as implied by the book's subtitle, *Metaphor and Guided Imagery for Psychotherapy and Healing*, he uses metaphor to heal, not specifically make place as Steinem's and my guided visualization did. Nevertheless, his therapeutic approach also has implications for place-making. Different from traditional "talk therapy," Battino guides the client through a metaphoric story as part of the therapeutic process.[29] During this process, while the conscious mind follows the story's plot, it's the patient's deeper, unconscious mind the therapist aims to access.[30]

The metaphors Rubio uses in the plot of the story are mirrors reflecting our inner images of self, life, and others.[31] For example, Battino reads patients a script wherein the notion of "building a house"[32] is a metaphor for building of self. A portion of that script reads:

A house full of places,
Empty spaces,
To be filled
And transformed
To meet the needs,
The desires,

Of those who choose
To live within,
Within oneself,
To weather the storms,
To work on ideas
To let the wind wander[33]

Each script's words are carefully chosen to elicit images, ideas, affects, and urges[34] not otherwise accessible via the conscious mind. This metaphor therapy[35] guided metaphor technique accesses a primordial place—one which, like dreams, has a deeper, magical, transformative power.[36]

Based on such visualization, Battino then coaxes patients to envision their future, to think about their life-journey by asking, "How would you change your evolving life's story? What would it be different so that you become who you want to be? What will be the form of these changes?[37]

He follows up by asking, "What particular healing images do you sense would work for you?"[38] Of relevance here is that Battino often suggests that clients "restructure or rewrite your story in some artistic medium"[39] since by doing so, "this as-if new story has a way of becoming real."[40] In asking patients to rewrite their self-story, he doesn't specifically suggest that patients use the medium of *design* as the Zaltmans, Gloria Steinem, and I did. Yet, since both scientific findings and more subjective, therapeutic techniques point to the power of place to transform, why not harness the power of healing metaphors to work such magic? After all, I now still believe the greatest metaphor of all remains the "house as symbol of self."

With this in mind, I've hung a wallpaper called *Obsidian*[41] on my dining room wall. I think I should call it a work of art rather than a wallpaper. I was transfixed by its amorphous, swirling pattern. I studied its blue repeat, and imagined I was climbing an azurite mountain in a Chinese landscape painting. I imagined myself walking through potent gray clouds and intermittent green clearings. I climbed calmly, intensely.

In sacred space,
Everything is done
So that the environment
Becomes a metaphor.[42]

This *Obsidian* imagery suggested my life-journey upward. Did a woman design this *Obsidian* wallpaper? I did some digging and found that the designer *was* a female. She deliberately created the wallpaper's imagery to be "strata-like"—derived from geology, precious stones, rock formations—with an overall open-ended visual quality that could be read as a landscape.[43] Fittingly, azurite is known as the "stone of heaven." Is it so named because it aids in the pursuit of our "heavenly self."? Each day as I grow older, I glance at that scene to remind myself to continue ever-upward on a life path full of new adventures and discoveries.

**Obsidian wallpaper
in the author's dining room.**
Photograph by the author.
Anthology Obsidian wallpaper
by Harlequin Wallpapers.

Esther Sternberg MD.
Photograph
by Kris Hanning.

Esther Sternberg, MD

When it comes to healing-place and stories, if you want more proof that research about feeling + neuroscience can be applied, look no further than to neuroimmunologist Esther Sternberg. Although an MD, not an architect or neuroscientist, she's a model for those determined to interweave disciplines to achieve a greater good. A writer as well as a scientist, she's a woman who has designed her life and work in a way that balances her objective and subjective sides. Sternberg's two books, *The Balance Within: The Science Connecting Health and Emotions*[1] and *Healing Spaces: The Science of Place and Well-Being*,[2] became the "go-to" tomes for those interested in creating health by design.

Of course I was intrigued! I wanted to learn what prompted her to journey down her unique road and if, on the way, she used her objective or subjective sides to create her own soothing home. Then, too, I thought I might convert her to Design Psychology since she wrote the following about the ways past-place memories and sense of self are inextricably entwined:

Memory of events and places is...crucial to our sense of self. ...All of your childhood memories, all of the memories you acquire every day of your life—what you have done, where you have done it, and how you felt while doing it—get stuck together. The collection in its entirety tells you who you are. If your memories start to fade, so do your sense of place and your sense of self. Start losing them and you lose a little bit of yourself with each memory that disappears.[3]

I got my chance to probe Sternberg's own self-place memories at a Healthcare Design Conference in Las Vegas[4] where she was due to speak about healing spaces. Little did I know when I approached her that we had both faced similar life-crises and both used imagery and environments to help heal others as well as help ourselves.

To me there's no less soothing place than the Las Vegas Strip. In order to meet with Sternberg, who'd become the darling of the healthcare design world, I had to weave my way past the Strip's amblers and gamblers and step into the huge, noisy food hall where she sat. Sternberg, a professionally dressed woman in her fifties, greeted me with a friendly, open smile that put me at ease. She began by asking me about Design Psychology rather than by boasting about her own theories or accomplishments.

I described my passionate belief that our design sensibilities come from our childhood memories of past-place, which we re-work (replicate and/or reject) when creating spaces. Having watched her PBS documentary[5] about her personal journey to a Greek village, an environment she believed had helped heal her physical/emotional illness, I commented to her:

> *Beyond just utilizing past-place memories, I've begun to wonder if design that tells the story of our past, present, and future might have a therapeutic effect. You used your environment in a therapeutic way. Similarly, I'm exploring how we can make therapeutic places to move us through the life-passages inherent in all lives—our journeys through the "Ds" of death of a loved one, divorce, disease, and even disaster, for example.*

Sternberg "got" Design Psychology instantly and replied:

> *That's fantastic. Well, I definitely hit all of those! I had arthritis, death, divorce. I didn't have disaster although, yes, I did. My mother died in '97. I moved into the house in '97 and then in 2001 there was 9/11. ...I went through all of this stress from the four biggies: job stress, divorce, moving, loss of a loved one, and death of a loved one in quick succession. Four months after my father had died of this long, debilitating Parkinson's and Alzheimer's-like illness, my mother was diagnosed with breast cancer. Five years later she died of breast cancer so it was a long ten-year period of this extended stress, and then the divorce in the middle of it, were all huge stressors.*

I wanted to hear Sternberg's whole heroine story. She continued by telling me about the Washington, DC home that she'd purchased and renovated. Although I wasn't taking her through my Design Psychology exercises, she drew on memory, metaphor, and emotion to make connections and arrive at insights about her self and place. For example, I learned that from the moment she occupied the house, it had symbolic meaning for Sternberg and her mother:

> *The day I moved into my new house in Washington, DC, I got a call telling me to go back to Montreal as it was the last days of my mother's life. It was very important to my mother when I moved into this new house that I actually had a house. She was always very concerned. In her generation, a divorced woman lost their income and prestige.*

> *I kept telling her, "I'm a doctor! I can always see patients if I can't do research!" But to her—knowing that I had a house—it was really important to her to know that I was settled. When I got that call, I got my camera (and this was before digital cameras) and went walking around the house—walked into the front door taking pictures, walked in the back and took pictures of everything.*

> *Then I got to Montreal. It was February and there was a terrible snowstorm. I went to see my mother in the hospital. I got her settled in and then walked down the hill in this terrible snowstorm to one of those one-hour photo developers and got the pictures*

developed. I walked back up the hill and laid them out on the hospital room tray table in order, as if you are walking in the front door. If you come in that door, here's the kitchen, here's the living room, here's the dining room.

How insightful of Sternberg to realize that she should brave a snowstorm in order to show her mother those photos, not just tell her in words about the new house. I wondered if her "scientist self" had logically deduced that a picture was worth a thousand words or if she just had acted on instinct and emotion, knowing how best to connect deeply with her mom. Sternberg continued:

She clearly was trying to visualize in her mind and then she said something that I didn't understand until after she died, "My dining room furniture will look really good in your dining room. She had always said she was never moving out of her house. To her, her house was very important. She'd lived there, I guess, for forty-five years.

It was extremely important to her because she had lost everything in the war. The family left Romania in 1938. They had to leave the home. So, to her, home and roots in a place were really important and she said if she ever gets to a point that she can't live in her house—then she doesn't want to live.

Clearly for Sternberg's mother, the house symbolized safety and security after her traumatic experiences in her Romanian homeland. It was only after Sternberg's father died, in fact, that Sternberg learned that he had been in a concentration camp. Thus, on Sternberg's mother's deathbed, it was understandable that she wanted her daughter to be safe and secure. As Sternberg explained, the passing down of furniture symbolized that kind of continuity:

I should have realized when she said, "My furniture will look really good in your dining room," that she knew she was going to die. Otherwise, why would her dining room furniture come into my dining room? I didn't realize that until after—or maybe I didn't want to hear it until after. But to her, the home...she must have recognized something about my new home that made her know that I'd be comfortable in it. Maybe she recognized that it was familiar to both of us and maybe that helped her die in peace.

Of course, for women of Sternberg's mom's generation, the house was their primary domain. Sternberg added, "She didn't work outside the home. She was the wife of a professor and doctor. She traveled around the world with my father when he gave lectures." I was intrigued when Sternberg then mentioned that, nevertheless, her mother, "At various times in her life...was a sculptress." Sternberg furthermore explained, "She was an oil painter and, at the end of her life, she wrote books."

Like Mother, like daughter? Putting the puzzle pieces together, it seemed no wonder that Sternberg had become a doctor/scientist given her father's profession, yet also become a writer given her mother's creative work. Sternberg explained:

The gifts my father and mother left to me were the way they lived and saw the world: my father, the scientist and physician; my mother the artist and, in later years, the writer. My father taught me always to question, confirm, and analyze. My mother taught me "to see a world in a grain of sand," and to "view every sunset as if it were my last." They both taught me to rejoice in life, to notice and appreciate every flower, and to delight in mountain views and sunsets.[6]

Thus, through these different ways of knowing, rather than reject the scientist or artist side of herself, she stood balanced in her being.

Still, as Sternberg continued, I realized that the memories and emotions that resided in her psyche guided her search for home. In fact, I learned that she had re-created her mother's home in her new DC residence. Sternberg, herself, began to recognize ways her environmental family tree unconsciously influenced her:

I kept saying I was looking for a certain kind of house in a certain part of Northwest, DC, but I couldn't find anything. Then I walked into this house in a different neighborhood...and immediately said, "Okay. This is it." Probably [because it was like my] mother's house—walkable, very close to public transportation where you have cafes, etc.—very European.

Ironically, given her training as an immunologist, Sternberg developed severe arthritis after her mother passed away. Thus the physician needed to heal herself. At this crossroads in her life:

My neighbors invited me to go to Greece. Why did I go? They were strangers...My mother had just died and my father had died several years before. So suddenly I was without parents. A couple came to the door and they had accents—not exactly the same as my parents accents, but European accents. They brought food that was exactly like my mother's cooking. Even though they were strangers, they were familiar people. It was as if my parents had come to the door and said, "Come with us." On my neighbor's part, they must have recognized something in me (even though they didn't know my background) that seemed familiar.

The very important thing was that I felt I began to heal in Greece—again because it was a familiar environment. I was suddenly steeped in this village that for me seemed familiar because of my memories from childhood because it was the same food. ...I've never gone back to Romania and never wanted to because my family had left in such awful circumstances but to me Greece was home. I felt very much at home.

Beyond familiarity, Sternberg believed that the power of sound, views of nature, and aromas in Greece had helped heal her own physical/emotional illness. This confirmed for her the profound impact of the multi-sensory environment on well-being. For me it confirmed how healing such transcendent environments can be, especially ones with positive past associations. Given her own insight, when

Sternberg returned back from Greece, she consciously added sensory elements to her home's landscaping that also had the power to heal. She explained:

I put a jasmine tree and a gardenia tree on the deck to remind me of the fragrance of the lemon and orange blossoms in Greece. Especially in the summer, I would stand out there and I inhale the fragrance of the jasmine tree in the night air and it would bring me back to Greece but also to older memories I have of childhood. ...My mother had a mock-orange tree in the backyard and it had the same kind of smell.

The other thing was—we used to go down to Miami Beach—in the winter my grandmother used to go down there and when I visited her, I loved the smell of the orange blossoms. I added my trees purposely because when I inhale their fragrance, I feel so much at peace.

In fact, it was when Sternberg first moved into her DC house, that she decided to rebuild her deck. Only later did she realize that the decisions she made about the deck's design were unconscious re-creations of her mother's home:

There was a beautiful old holly bush off [my] back deck. The architect said, "We can make your deck wider. We just need to get rid of the tree. I said, "Absolutely no way! You are not going to take this holly away!"

I didn't realize when I told the architect how wide to make the deck, I was saying the same thing my mother had said when she put in her deck. In her case there was a beautiful old lilac tree that she didn't want moved to make the deck wider. On my deck I put in quarry stone and wrought iron rails and a spiral staircase.

My mother had wrought iron railings and a spiral staircase but I didn't know I was recreating my mother's deck until I was finished and there it was and I said, "Oh my God! I just made my Mother's deck!". ...So maybe one reason I felt at home the minute I walked into the house was these elements that made me feel at home.

Then, too, Sternberg added a sunroom that was, perhaps, a metaphor for her healing process, just as her mother had created a sunroom as part of her healing process. Sternberg explained:

My mother always wanted a sunroom. She finally started building a sunroom, which ended up being way too small. She wanted some outdoor space so the sunroom had to be even smaller. She finally started building it when my father first became ill, of course not realizing that he was so sick.

I am sure it was part of her own therapy. She had to get in the sun. ...That was very important to her. She was always complaining about the fact that [the sunroom] was too small but it was too small because she made it that way. The sunroom had to fit on the deck that she had made too narrow because of the lilac tree!

So what did I do? I broke through the wall of the dining room and put in a sunroom. I didn't think of this until now but the architect said, "You can have a bigger sunroom if you use two-thirds instead of one third of the deck. I opted for a sunroom that was a third [of the space] because I wanted to have more outdoor space.

Sternberg laughed, thinking about how she'd replicated her mother's sunroom. She reflected, "So, again, I made the same decision my mother did. I'm not sorry about it because I love sitting outside but, in retrospect, it's the same decision she had made."

Immersed by now in our discussion, she commented, "This is very, very interesting! This is great! This is so much fun!"

It wasn't just that Sternberg unconsciously drew from memory of past place. She unknowingly replicated her mother's unconscious process of using design in a *therapeutic* way. Both mother and daughter made changes to their home during moments of life passages. Moreover, these home's transformations, laden with underlying meaning and emotion, acted as metaphors that helped each woman achieve well-being.

Toward the end of our discussion, Sternberg made a final connection between her home's renovation and her own healing process given the traumatic event that occurred during that time:

Oh yes, 9/11. I live in Washington, DC across from the Israeli Embassy and several other embassies including Jordan and the United Arab Emirates. The whole Middle East was across the street from me, so it was a very, very tough time.

My deck and sunroom were still under construction, and I remember climbing up this ladder knowing that this wasn't the smartest thing in the world to do and just sitting out on the half-done deck and thinking, "At least I'm building something as opposed to tearing down." I was very clear in my mind about that. It made me feel a great deal of comfort to know that I am contributing to creating and building as opposed to tearing down the porch. So it gave me comfort in times of disaster.

In her career, too, Sternberg experienced a similar gratification:

When I wake up in the morning, I don't have to ask myself, "Is what I'm doing worth it?" I know that I am helping people. I know that when I was in medical practice, I knew that I was helping people. At every stage of my career, I knew that I was helping people. That always gave me—I wouldn't say "comfort"—strength?

Like all pioneers with a mission, Sternberg recognized the wider implications of her work:

Now where I see my career going is in terms of health and the space around you. How does the environment in which we live—whether it's the immediate environment or everything that we sense/perceive through each of our senses—what we hear, smell, and touch moving through the environment, how does that affect your memory and your emotions, which then affect hormones and nerve chemicals that affect your immune system?

And then in terms of the larger world, there's the larger environment: How does the green environment affect health? So that's really where I'm going; that environment mind/body connection. I think it has tremendous implications for personal health, for wellness, for intervention, for public health policy, for hospital design, workplace design, urban design, and for people's individual, local environment design. It has tremendous importance for international policy in developing countries and emerging economies.

Overall, then, Sternberg was seeking to make connections between the environment/self, emotions/mind/body, and her personal experience and the wider world. Hers is a scientist's "connected knowing" based on *feeling* as well as scientific data from her so-meaningful research.[7] Thus, she serves as a model for other women wanting balance in their being as well as for those creating diverse, human-focused careers.

PART III:

Applying
Design Psychology:
Case Studies

CHAPTER 6:
Women Make Space

I learned so much from Esther Sternberg and my own illness about the science of the mind and our subjective experience when it comes to healing by design. In truth, all of the stories from Julia Morgan's to my own convinced me that there's an unconscious, emotional aspect to place-making that needs to be addressed.

Given all I've learned, I believe:

- We can create transcendent places that make us feel "alive" and tuned into our human, rather than mechanistic, experience of the world.
- Such transcendent design based on our lived experience combined with place-making that gives voice to our most liberated sense of self can act as a catalyst for emotional well-being.
- Design elements that incorporate the use of "place as a metaphor for self" as a therapeutic tool have the potential to help people envision a positive future.
- The most balanced place-making approach is one informed both by objective evidence as well as the subjective sensibility historically associated with women/interior design that's too often been disparaged.

So now, by way of further illustration and with that imbalance to redress, I'm going to highlight how other women I worked with *consciously* used Design Psychology to create interiors in a subjective, transformative sense. After all, if we can remember and revel in dappled light, cool sheets, the scent of orange blossoms or a zillion other past-place memories that shoot like glowing stars through our unconscious, why not harness such imagery when place-making?

Over the years I've led both professionals and non-professionals through my Design Psychology process so that their environmental lived experience could unfold. Those who went through my exercises were 1) participants in my online and in-person group workshops like the one I conducted at BCRC; 2) individual clients wanting to design their residence or healing space; 3) students enrolled in my year-long training program learning how to use the Design Psychology process in their practice.

Those reaching out to me were mostly interior designers or psychologists. As a Design Psychologist, this makes sense to me because both professions deal with "interior" space. Interestingly, a whopping 93% of all my workshop participants were females; all but one of those who enrolled in my year-long training program were females too. Seventy-eight percent of all workshop attendees scored as F (Feeling) types.[1] Such data continues to suggest to me that there's a *feeling* way that these (and other?) woman *know*, which they want to embrace and express through place design.

To show, and not just tell you how Design Psychology can be applied, what follows is a series of case studies. The first case study is that of "Katya", [2] a Sydney-based interior designer and building biologist[3] (originally trained in interior design) who enrolled in my Design Psychology training program. I include Katya's story in full because it's a particularly unique account of the how the *institutional* oppression of her native Russia affected not only her well-being, but the cultural/emotional landscape of Russian citizenry overall during a tumultuous time of change in the 1990s. Likewise, she insightfully reflects on how, once living in Australia, she use Design Psychology to overcome her own *internalized* oppression—to find her woman's voice and greater self-esteem. Throughout, she relied on the metaphor of home to heal her self.

Besides the text of her story, I've included visuals of the exercises she completed to show you how the Design Psychology process proceeds, step by step. I hope this written and visual road map entices you further to explore and use your life's journey as a touchstone for design.

Overall, I hope all of the case studies show you how Design Psychology can:
- Help you explore the rich environmental stories of your life
- Raise your awareness of ways your 'self' and place are intertwined
- Suggest how you can design places that mirror your best 'self'
- Encourage you to use human-centered place-making tools to envision a positive future

. . . .

"One Woman's Journey from Oppression to Self-Realization" by "Katya"

THE PAST

When I look back at my life I see a map. A map full of roads that I have traveled across the continents, cities full of experiences that I have lived, forests full of emotions that I have felt, busy intersections that I thought I never would cross, high mountains that I never imagined I would climb, oceans full of my fears, and rivers full of laughter that I have sailed. Undoubtedly, every experience of the map of my life has left its indelible imprint, forever informing and guiding my journey of trying to figure out how best to dwell on Earth and live a life of meaning and beauty.

What led me to where I am now? To Sydney, the place that I now call home, that gives me a sense of comfort and belonging, the place that is on the other side of the world from where I was born. What influenced the rich texture and substance of my life map—the very fabric of my sense of self?

I began to answer these questions by completing the first two exercises in the *Design Psychology Toolbox*.

Exercise 1: Environmental Family Tree Exercise

Katya's Environmental Family Tree Exercise opened the first chapter of her environmental autobiography, the story of her journey forward to a more liberated culture and sense of self.

Homes of My Ancestors

Your Environmental Family Tree

I took note of what aspects of my ancestors' places stood out for me:

- Grandfather's Place
- A village: surrounded by garden with a lot of free space
- Village life, full of aromas related to the garden: berries, fruit, bees
- Connection to earth: earthy aromas of the village, grounding
- Endearing, soul-touching, star gazing sitting on the porch
- Tasting poppies when they flowered and dried—food for the soul
- Fulfillment of a lot of sensory needs: colors and textures—outlook
- Feeling at ease there, comfortable

When I completed my *Environmental Timeline* more past place memories flooded in:

Exercise 2: Environmental Timeline Exercise

Katya's Environmental Timeline Exercise acted as a catalyst inviting her to track the homes she journeyed through.

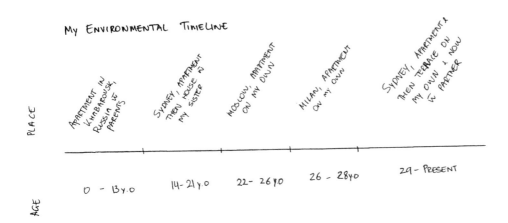

After I completed my *Environmental Timeline* I made notes about the houses that were my favorite:

Coogee, Australia (favorite house)

- Private and secluded, but open and airy, large scale, spacious
- Connection to the land, connected to the earth, aromas, colors, light, birds, and in view of the ocean
- I can see a lot of spaces: limitless view, open lookout, and even though it's large I feel comfortable, cozy, and secure. It looks large on the outside but it is very comfortable and cozy on the inside and allows for privacy

Blakehurst House

- Serene, greenery, open space: it felt safe and nurturing
- But was too far from resources: felt isolated, the setting wasn't lively enough, felt too far

Right away I began to see the similarities and differences between my PAST and PRESENT house. My house now is surrounded by land. I am connected to garden/nature/land; large and spacious yet private and cozy, feeling safe and secure, fulfilling to the senses.

Exercise 3: Mental Map Exercise

The Mental Map Exercise helped Katya identify her transcendent experience of past childhood place.

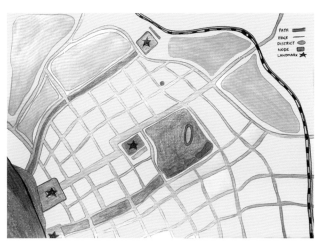

Drawing by Katya.

When I did the *Mental Map Exercise*, I remembered the town that I grew up in and how I used to spend time by the river and went to the park and its main square. These memories became my mental map—a symbolic image of place I carry in my mind. Going to the river with my friends was a significant positive thing that five or ten of us kids would do almost every week. I remember how free and easy I felt, spending hours there with them. I could be myself there uninhibited and fearless, without my parents or adults watching my every move. It was a time away from home where the atmosphere was often tense and emotionally challenging. Time spent by the river provided me with emotional refuge and space to explore. We would spend hours there, roaming around little nooks and crannies, picking up sticks and stones, playing hide and seek.

The one-and-a-half-hour walk to the river and back was in itself a memorable adventure that represented a psychological transition from the world of "control" to the world of "freedom." I cherished every minute of it. We would walk along one of the pedestrian boulevards that ran from the embankment to the east side of town along each side of the main street. These boulevards were wide streets lined with tall trees on each side and benches located strategically along the way so one could sit down, have a rest, and enjoy the calmness emanating from the trees.

Walking along these wide, beautiful streets felt somewhat enchanting. It was almost like journeying through a well-maintained forest in the middle of the city to get to the place where magic happened—the river. The expansiveness and coziness provided by trees, benches and little kiosks that sold ice cream along the way felt very nurturing and embracing. Walking along those streets replenished my enthusiasm and curiosity. Indeed, these surroundings provided much comfort as a child.

Exercise 4: Favorite Childhood Place Visualization Exercise

*Doing the **Guided Visualization Exercise** helped Katya probe more deeply into her transcendent, emotional connection to past place and retrieve sensory memories, touchstones for future design.*

Next, when I closed my eyes and did the *Favorite Childhood Place Visualization Exercise* I returned to my grandfather's house, which I could remember in great sensory detail. I took notes on what I visualized:

> *Berry hedges: feels homey*
> *I feel safe and relaxed*
> *Connection to land*
> *Fruitful, useful garden in Grandfather's place*
> *Edible garden, lovely aromas from edible trees*
> *I would like to have berry hedges, a veggie patch, and vines*

. . . .

Boxed Into Bleakness

Despite these fond memories, when I was growing up in the '80s and '90s in the post-Soviet Russia, the socio-political climate of the country wasn't very stable. Russia was in the process of changing from a communist dictatorship into a democracy. Only much later, in my adult years, did I start making sense of what was happening during those times. Even as a child I could sense the uncertainty in everyday life and mistrust in the system that left everyone feeling anxious, reserved, and suspicious of each other. As kids (at least in my family) we were encouraged to be like everybody else, not to speak up too much, stand out, or draw attention, due to fear of attracting unnecessary attention from authorities. These values of suspicion, secrecy, and ostracism were strongly reinforced by the small, simple, box-like apartments we all lived in. These mass-produced apartment buildings dominated the Russian landscape in '70s, '80s, and '90s. They looked the same inside and out. Most were filled with similar-looking furniture. These gray, box-like spaces kept everyone boxed in, compartmentalized, and separated, both literally and metaphorically. They reinforced the culture of mistrust, privacy, and austerity. As an adult I recognize that, undoubtedly, as I was growing up, my larger surroundings and relationships I had with them also left distinctive emotional imprints on my identity.

Breaking Down the Walls of Austerity
or Life Beyond Limits

My pre-teen years played out in a remarkably different culture, which also, undoubtedly, influenced the landscape of my psyche. In 1991, when Soviet Union fell apart and I was nine years old, Russia suddenly switched from a position of "everything is forbid-

Soviet style high-rise apartment building typical of the 1990s.
Shutterstock.

den" to "nothing is off limits." The mantra was "grab as much as you can." Money (which up until then had meant nothing) now meant everything. In theory, this all sounds fantastic: freedom, a fresh start, and unlimited possibilities. In practice, however, it all became too much, too soon, and came out a bit twisted. The complete collapse of the system created a vacuum that was quickly filled by an avalanche of the new: new things to buy and discover—new music, TV, sexuality, and identity.

Everything new flooded the country and overnight there was paradox of choice. Some were taking advantage of chaos and getting rich fast. Others were getting deeper into poverty and barely making ends meet. Crime sprees skyrocketed, drug-culture flourished, infrastructure collapsed, food shortages became a norm. The whole country was going through a cultural identity crisis. After having been denied self-exploration and expression for years behind the Iron Curtain, everyone was desperate to find their own sense of self, separate from the state and from each other.

This shift in ideology from "everything is forbidden" to "nothing is off limits" was quickly reflected in the design of living spaces. Tired of the sameness and grayness of place that boxed in their personalities, and motivated by desire to seek a more physically comfortable life, people began tearing down walls in their homes and adorning them with objects they thought represented beauty, luxury, style, and comfort—a Western ideal of a light, open, and beautiful home.

Most of the time the result was a bit bizarre. A typical renovated apartment of the post-Soviet time had white walls, gadgets, and some modern furniture. However, it also could include Persian carpets on the floor (and walls), lots of elaborate decorations, and even furniture à la Ludwig XXV chairs with the gold-plated curved legs and armrests. Legend has it that some even had golden door handles and golden urinals. It was an unstoppable blast of gluttonous creative energy born out of decades of visual-, material-, and self-oppression.

Our home got filled with objects and furniture that looked like they came out of a weird and wonderful treasure chest. We had tapestries on walls, gilded furniture, colorful Persian rugs, and wooden stumps for seats—all mixed together with remnants of Soviet-inspired wallpaper with stylized floral motifs and rich, velvet curtains. It was an explosion of styles mixed all in one little apartment; you could call it eclectic or hectic and confused.

Then, in 1997, when I was fifteen years old, I moved from Russia to Australia with my older sister. My parents stayed in Russia for another couple of years until my mum came over in 2004 after my parents divorced. Having grown up for the most part in the standardized post-Soviet reality, I was shocked to see how different the "other" reality was. People were open and friendly. There was no fear, no suspicion, no standoffishness, no strictness. It felt light and pleasantly devoid of drama. For someone like me, who was quite "boxed-in" and very shy, this was quite a significant change. At first I found that I was heavily influenced by that "leave me in my shell" mentality that sprang from an underlying mistrust of others and sense that I was not safe in the world, that people are out there to get me, which I inherited from the collective unconscious of the Soviet culture. Despite this, and my cautious and reserved personality, I felt very emotionally safe in my new home even though I was miles away from my parents and everything that was remotely familiar.

Later in my twenties I traveled a lot and, although I thought I de-Sovietized myself, I always chose to live alone. Most places I lived in were apartments similar to what I grew up in with distinct functional separation of spaces. They tended to reinforce that familiar feeling of isolation and detachment. Did I pick them subconsciously trying to re-create my childhood home? Was I keeping myself isolated and invisible to the rest of the world by living in those places because that's what felt familiar?

Coming Into My Own

Like my relationship with myself, my relationship with my home has been through a lot of ups and downs. At first, when I moved in four years ago, I felt like it was not pretty enough, not perfect enough, not comfortable enough, most likely fueled by my sense of perfectionism and feelings of not being enough myself, which I have inherited from my upbringing.

So, for a while, I imposed my aesthetic on my home constantly re-arranging furniture, bringing new objects in, changing curtains, re-hanging pictures. Although I was constantly unhappy with the result, reflecting my inner dissatisfaction with my own self, it felt like the home enjoyed my attention and fussiness. This dissatisfaction with myself and unwillingness to accept who and where I was at that moment in time soon grew into a feeling of hopelessness: I felt that I would never be able to make it right and that this home was not right for me. There were just too many things that I couldn't change because it was a home that I rented, not owned.

I grew apathetic toward my home and started concentrating on personal and spiritual development using my house only as a physical shelter. The interesting thing is

Interior of Russian apartment in the Post-Soviet era.
Shutterstock.

that I think my home felt that and tried to "lock me out" by letting me forget my keys at least five times within a period of two months, which had never happened before.

Like any relationship that is going through a rough patch, it was bringing everything that was unconscious up to the surface for me to acknowledge, accept, and heal. I was becoming more and more impatient and picky. Previously, a comfortable and peaceful environment, it now seemed restrictive and claustrophobic. It didn't feel like my refuge anymore. It wasn't soothing or joyful to be there and it felt like my home was saying to me, "Since you don't like me anymore, I don't care about you either and I want you to leave."

At that time I wasn't in a position to buy a house, so moving to another place meant I would be renting again. Logically, it didn't make any sense to escape from my then-reality into another one that would probably bring the same issues up to the surface. Deep down I grew attached to it and was reluctant to leave.

It was my impatience with myself and unwillingness to accept myself just as I was that lay at the core of this crisis. My home put a magnifying glass on that inner conflict and brought it to light. There was no denying it anymore or dwelling in the emotional debris of blaming my parents. It was time to quietly sit with what is and let myself heal. Of course, it didn't happen overnight since healing is an on-going process. However, in time, my hesitation about being where I was and dissatisfaction with what was present seemed to subside. Instead of focusing on everything that I didn't like about my home, I decided to turn my attention to what I wanted to see flourish and grow in my life—love, connection, wholeness, and wisdom.

Overall, similar to tearing down walls in those box-like apartments in Russia, I've felt my internal layout was being re-arranged by the many different places I lived in. I could see how I was becoming more open to free-flowing interaction, more communicative, and less rigid. I was tearing down the psychological barriers built in my childhood, and the places that I was choosing to live in were helping me do that. The more I explored my inner self, the easier it became to recognize how my positive place experiences were informing my present environmental choices. As I was looking for more freedom and expression of creativity, I was more attracted to settings that allowed me to be more of myself—like places that had closer connection to nature and were full of natural light.

For example, during this time, my home in Sydney was located within easy walking distance from the ocean where I went at least two or three times a week. The act of walking to the ocean and spending time there was very much reminiscent of my childhood walks to the riverfront. Similar to my childhood, this was where I felt at ease, spacious, clear, and calm. I reconnected with myself. It re-invigorated and inspired me every time, much like those boulevards and the river from my childhood.

I stopped alienating myself from my house and my reality and started reconnecting with myself. Interestingly, I didn't start with re-decorating the interior. Instead, I began tending to my neglected tiny garden by planting beautiful and fragrant flowers, finding some quirky plant pots, and placing them randomly throughout the garden. I hung some outside candle lights, bought two bright yellow cane chairs, got a compost bin, planted some herbs and veggies, and made a stone medicine wheel[1] in the courtyard at the back. Tending a garden slowly brought back the feelings of warmth, calmness, and connection with my home. I felt proud about this beautiful self-made environment.

I wasn't projecting my inner fears and anxieties onto my home anymore. Instead, I was re-establishing my sense of comfort and security in my own way. I am glad that I didn't escape from my uncomfortable feelings and instead decided to feel them. In a way, I feel like it helped me to come out of my shell of insecurities, to rebuild my inner strength, and start learning how to love myself.

THE PRESENT

I eventually came to study interior design and never looked back. And thus began my journey into exploring people-space relationship and pondering on my own sense of place. But it wasn't until I came across Design Psychology that I delved back into my childhood on a journey of re-discovering my own sense of home and learning how deeply we are connected with our environments—how they can affect our physical, mental, emotional, and spiritual well-being.

This was the beginning of search for my "place of the soul." In fact, during my Design Psychology studies, as a result of doing the *Ideal Place Exercise*, I devised an "Ideal Home" vision.

Exercise 5: Ideal Place Exercise

Katya used her positive associations with past place to envision her ideal home in the future.

My ideal home is my own home located near the ocean and not far from the forest. My home is my sanctuary; it is cozy and beautiful, grounding, filled with light, free-flowing, and nurturing. It expresses my own unique self, my connection with nature, my creativity, and is filled with joy, love, and vitality. It satisfies my need to be on my own and be a part of the community. It is built from healthy and natural materials and has a garden where I can grow vegetables and flowers. My home harmonizes my physical, emotional, and spiritual aspect of my being.

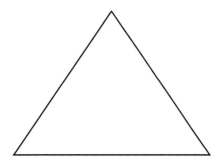

Gradually Katya began to create her own space that felt not only liberating but transcendent, too.

So now I might be in the same home I was two years ago, but I find that a lot has changed since then. I find that my aesthetic has changed—it became much more calm and subdued. I don't feel like I need to constantly stand out and express myself through a burst of colors and textures inside my home. I feel it quietly became my resting place, my refuge, my delight in being with what is. Nothing has to be perfect but rather tenderly cared for. I don't feel like I need to push my personality onto my home anymore, and that we have adjusted to accept and love each other just as we are.

Photograph by Katya.

Exercise 6: Special Objects Inventory Exercise[2]

*When doing the **Special Objects Inventory Exercise**, Katya identified special objects like her Medicine Wheel that reconnected her to transcendent, sensory memories of healing oases.*

In fact, the home that I live in today has a lot of what I envisioned as my ideal home. It is small, cozy, and nurturing; filled with objects that have meaning to me; and reflects my creativity and my unique journey thus far.

Coming from an interior design background, a visually pleasant aesthetic is very important to me. I like having beautiful objects and furniture in my home. I like looking at them and feeling inspired or remembering how I felt when they came into my life. Each one is filled with special meaning and memories that stem from a variety of emotional and physical experiences and journeys I have undertaken.

Looking at the interior of my home, one could easily say that it was very eclectic—with its over-sized blue velvet couch, large multi-colored rug, tall black second-hand wooden cupboard with a naked silhouette of a woman that I drew on its doors several years ago, a red oriental-inspired console with an Aboriginal painting hanging above it, and a small statue of Buddha sitting on top—each visually exciting and reflective of my personality.

The drawing Katya painted on her cupboard conveys the feeling of a woman who is more present and strong – less vulnerable.

Exercise 7: Personality and Place Exercise

*Results of the **Personality and Place Exercise** Katya completed suggested that she is a INFJ (Introverted, Intuitive, Feeling, Judging) personality type. Her Buddha expresses her introverted side, yet her wall tapestry exudes the feeling, "I am alive!" Photograph by Katya.*

The Future
Living and Working Together

Since most of the time I lived alone in my current home, I didn't have to share my space and worry about coming to terms with another's expression of self. It was all my individual space. This is starting to change as my new partner and I are thinking of moving in together. Still, when my partner started spending more time in my house and working some days of the week here as well, I found that I started feeling territorial.

Exercise 8: Environmental Sociogram Exercise

*By completing the **Environmental Sociogram Exercise** Katya became more conscious of her 'social need' for both privacy and connection.*

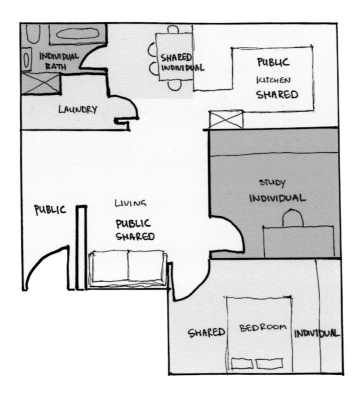

Drawing by Katya.

Yet, since I want him to feel welcome—and help see him through this transition as smoothly as possible—I cleaned out the study, which he now uses as his office. He re-arranged the room the way he liked it as a personal and work space.

On this journey of transitioning from being single to becoming a couple and sharing a home together, I can't help but think how our individual environmental histories will inform this transition. My partner's background is very different to mine. Unlike my ambivalent memories of childhood home, my partner remembers his childhood home with affection and care. We also grew up in two different countries with very different cultural, social, and political climates on opposite sides of the world.

Despite our different backgrounds, we share similarities too. I guess, you could say we are "in training" for figuring out how to create a shared, loving, and comfortable home for both of us to live in. Making a home together, similar to other life transitions, is never clear and simple but nevertheless an important step in one's exploration of sense of self. As our interior self changes and evolves, the interior and exterior environments of our homes change and evolve as well.

Exercise 9: Home as Self-Actualization Exercise

Katya used the Pyramid of Needs to envision what transcendent liberating design elements she wanted in the future.

MY IDEAL HOME PLACE - FUTURE TRIANGLE

My ideal home place is:
a beautiful, large, airy, open, sunlit and well-connected house that is also private, cosy and relaxing. It's an endearing place that touches my soul, where I feel safe, at ease, grounded and connected to earth and nature at large. It is well-organised and looked after, and where everything has its own place. It is filled with art that I absolutely love and that represents the essence of my nature. My home is emotionally-supportive, enriching and nourishing to my soul.

Home Setting
Surburban, next to the ocean/beach,
on top of the hill, no neigbours - privacy
beautiful garden with fruit-bearing trees
open space, land, vastness, lookout/view

House
Large house, big rooms, high ceilings, large windows overlooking the garden
Sense of space, well-connected rooms
Attic with a small balcony and windows to look at the sky and make art

Private and spacious - no clutter;
there is a place for everything and everything has its own place,
calming and grounding with soft pastel colours, light green, light greys, whites,
soft purples and accents of colour through art and objects
modern/clean lines yet rich with textures;
sunroom/dining room; balcony overlooking the garden

Objects
filled with beautiful & meaningful obejcts/works of art, attention to detail,
interesting objects that are complimentary to the house and thoughtfuly
placed; art/paintings that give a sense of nourishment and connection, only essential pieces that represent my personality and are emotionally supportive,
warmth of timber, well-planted/organised garden
private seating areas on wrap-around verandah
Art on walls, beautiful & comfortable furniture couches

I look forward to the next chapter of my life journey and the treasures (lessons) that it will bring. I think that doing Design Psychology exercises made it clearer for me how our homes are expressions of our inner selves, our beliefs, our desires, and our challenges. I think that by doing the Design Psychology work I have realized that our homes are not destinations or "things" to be achieved or accomplished, and they don't have to be perfect or complete. Our homes are stories in the making of our lives and, if we are flexible, we can learn a lot from them.[3]

My Design Psychology Blueprint

The mood board Katya made to accompany her written Design Psychology Blueprint helped guide her creation of her Ideal Future Home.
Mood board by Katya.

Transformation by Design

The case studies I present next are shorter snapshots of ways Design Psychology worked for other women wishing to transform their interior space. Of particular interest is that each woman was experiencing a different life-passage while on her self/place journey:

- *Olga*, a home-style writer whom I mentored, was separating from her childhood environment and creating her first home.
- *Sarah*, a clinical psychologist and a student in my Design Psychology training program, writes about a case study she completed during her mentorship. She worked with *Maribel*, a single parent, who wished to make a solid, cozy nest for herself and her young girls.
- *Jennifer*, my client, was about to become an empty nester. She completed a home addition using Design Psychology as a way of welcoming in her wider community.
- *Suzan*, also a clinical psychologist, enrolled in my training program. She worked with "*Nary*," a second-generation immigrant seeking to move house and find home. Of special interest is that Suzan embedded the Design Psychology process in her therapeutic, not design, practice.
- *Binnie*, my client, needed a new place to grieve, recover, and make a new life after the death of her beloved husband.

After going through the *Design Psychology Toolbox*,[1] some of these women went on to make design choices on their own. They selected interior design elements— colors, furniture, special objects, etc., as recommended in their Design Psychology Blueprint. Others hired architects or interior designers who used their client's Design Psychology Blueprint of recommendations as a guide for making place. A few hired me to help them carry out their place-making plan. No matter what the final design route, every one of these Transformation by Design stories highlights how these women used Design Psychology to become more aware of their own lived experience and of ways they could translate that experience into transcendent, liberating space.

After each of their vignettes, I provide specific suggestions to others going through a similar life-stage about how to use Design Psychology as a catalyst for well-being. Those tips are collectively based on the many other clients' stories that I've heard over the years. No matter what stage you are passing through, feel free to use those suggestions in conjunction with doing the Design Psychology **He/She/They Oasis Exercises** specific to this book, although adapted from the original *Design Psychology Toolbox of Exercises*.[2] Just go to www.designpsychology.net/DWL.pdf to access the adapted exercises. You can complete the exercises in the sequence indicated in the 'Suggestions' section after each of the case studies below.

Lived Experience: BECOMING

**My Environmental Autobiography
by Olga Strużyna**

THE PAST

I was born in Warsaw, the capital of Poland. I lived there with my twin sister and parents in an apartment until I was twenty-eight. When I think back to those years, I realize I had no privacy, since I shared my room with my sister. Even in my early childhood, for example, my only private place was my drawer in kindergarten. Then, too, my privacy often was disrupted by my mother and grandmother. Someone was always checking on me. I remember that one of them read my diary. Then, too, my mother didn't have housekeeping skills. She was a collector, but had so many things in the house you couldn't admire any of them.

Luckily, the district where I lived was away from the city center so I had places where I could wander. I remember small shops—ice cream, bakery, and shoe shops. In the nearby park we sunbathed in summer and went skiing or sledding downhill in the winter. Nearby, separating my house from railroad tracks, there was a green belt full of bushes and trees. Here my friends and I collected flowers or herbs for drying, or snails and ladybirds. I always felt free and ready for adventure there. From these experiences I gained a still-deep need to be with nature.

In fact, when I did the Design Psychology *Guided Visualization Exercise*, I vividly remembered a house in nature—the transcendent bungalow of my mother's best friend, "Auntie Basia." It was a bungalow in the middle of the forest. It was quite small with only about two rooms but had lots of books and paintings. I used to go there between the ages of seven to twelve. It had a wonderful atmosphere with lots of trees outside, old furniture inside, and lots of food. I felt happy when I went there. I felt freedom! For the first time, I really *felt* deeply that I wanted to live close to nature.

Olga Strużyna.
Photograph by
Michał Przeździk.

129

Interior of Olga's aunt's house.
Photograph by Olga Strużyna.

Later, since I'd lived so long with my family and my twin sister, I wanted to spend time by myself. I made my own, first mature decision when I took a break from my university and went abroad to Amsterdam. There I lived in a house with no curtains on the windows, a big greenhouse, with farmland in the back and a garden in the front. I felt very comfortable there: calm, free, happy, close to the water and nature. By spending time without my mom and sister, I found myself.

The next year, after being depressed, I went to Holland for a second time. I worked in a restaurant. The owners treated me as a part of their family. They noticed me, accepted me, cared about me. I felt more important. I didn't need to play a role or be perfect.

THE PRESENT

When my grandmother died, she left me this apartment. I chose to live here because of what she represented to me: an honest, good person who liked things clean—not like in my mother's house. My grandmother was more of a mother to me than my real mother. Nevertheless, when my grandmother lived here, I never liked this apartment. It felt too small and full of unnecessary things. Her old furniture also wasn't very attractive. During our Design Psychology work, I realized that I didn't want her old furniture anymore. I bought new furniture and mixed it with the old pieces. Now I only have the few things I really need.

Still, this present home doesn't reflect my full personality. I do not feel free here, maybe because of the fact that it's still a small space. There were only two rooms, but I kicked the walls out and created an open space. Similarly, although in my neighborhood there are small shops, a church, etc., I'm more in the city center than before. That's not a good thing. I have no close contact with nature.

Wondering if I belong in this apartment, I thought I should become aware of what I was going through. I started to read *Some Place Like Home*[1] and Cooper Marcus's book.[2] Then, after one Design Psychology session, I realized that I still was stuck with "things." I decided to make changes step by step. I was a little afraid, but I liked it. Doing the *Ideal Place Exercise* helped me realize what type of home I wanted:

My ideal home is warm, cozy with magical atmosphere including artwork, candles, glass or crystal dishes and furniture that doesn't overcrowd. It has a garden where I can walk on the grass in my bare feet. Partly sunny, partly shady, it makes me and my guests feel that we never want to leave.

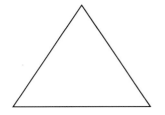

After writing this, while still sitting at my desk I thought, "This isn't my desk—it was my grandmother's desk." I had a lot of energy and couldn't sleep, so I started to rearrange the space. The place was a mess, which didn't make me feel good, but something kept me from changing it—from being open, free. I think it was an old part of myself, so I said to myself, "Can I clean out old papers and old junk? Yes! I can do this, but very slowly."

It has been very difficult for me to cut out the old part of me—what my mum wanted me to be—and to look to the future to create my own new family that would care about me. Nevertheless, I threw out objects like small ceramic figures from my mum, my grandmother's candlestick, etc., which reflected my family's taste, not mine.

THE FUTURE

Now I see that everything has a connection. I want to visit my Auntie Basia's house again. I want to take a photo of it because I think it's really quite important. It's so similar to what I want in the future. I'm not sure I can get a house like that, but, if I believe in that dream, why not? I have a piece of land. I am hoping to build a small summer house there. I now know how my future should look. I want to feel that my home is my place where people notice and respect me—where I can stand on my strong legs. I want to feel grass under my feet. It's time to open next chapter of my life. I am ready for it.

Olga's Aunt's PAST House.
Photograph by Olga Strużyna.

Olga's PRESENT House.
Photograph by Olga Strużyna.

. . . .

Five years later Olga wrote to me:

Now I am pregnant and have moved with my husband to the home I always dreamed about. It's a small house near the forest like the one where my auntie lived. (Do you remember it from the *Guided Visualization Exercise*?) This house is awesome. Maybe it's not exactly like my auntie's—but it's quite in my style now.

I am continuing to do work with Design Psychology. Sometime I run workshops. More recently I completed a project for a cancer hospital designing two day-rooms for cancer patients and their families, as well as a small part of their lawn. It was really great for me.

"Becoming" Place Suggestions:

(All exercises are available at www.designpsychology.net/DWL.pdf)

- Complete the *Environmental Family Tree Exercise # 1* to **raise your awareness about which self-place family patterns you want to repeat versus jettison**.
- Rather than obey mass media, parental, or other "authorities" who tell you how you should, ought, or must design, complete the *Women by Design Exercise #2* to **identify the self/home qualities of those you most admire. Decide if/how you want to combine those qualities with your own unique sense of self as you design.**
- Complete the *Oasis by Design Timeline Exercise #3* to **identify any oasis design qualities in your past homes that you want to recreate in your current and future home**.
- Complete the *Ideal Place Exercise #4* to **arrive at one life/place mission statement that serves as your North Star as you embark on the journey of your life/home change and growth.**
- Complete the *Favorite Childhood Place Visualization #5* to **retrieve the transcendent essence of a childhood place that you want to capture in any future design**.

Lived Experience: **NESTING**

Helping My Client Achieve a "Cultural Oasis"
by Sarah Seung-McFarland, Ph.D.

When I first started working with my client Maribel, she was dissatisfied with the state of her apartment, and did not feel like it was a true reflection of who she is or what she wanted to become. Maribel is a single mother with two lovely daughters and a rich Puerto Rican ancestry. She works in human resources by day, but also has a creative side she has not expressed as fully as she likes. She is in the process of switching to a career in interior design. So I set out to help her put together a creative home environment that can act as a backdrop to the life she wants to live.

Psychologist
Sarah Seung-MacFarland,
Ph.D. (right) with her
client Maribel Colon (left).
Photography by Sarah
Seung-MacFarland.

While conducting the exercises with Maribel, a number of themes came up. One major theme was self-expression—having a voice. Growing up, Maribel felt female voices were not always valued or well received. She wanted to ensure that both her and her daughters felt comfortable enough in the home to express their identity. At the same time, she wanted the home to have a masculine presence since a male does not live in the home. Thus, I recommended that the space celebrate strong Latina women but also embrace masculinity.

Another major theme was clutter. Maribel realized that clutter (i.e., having a bunch of paperwork and things piled up on the floor), a longstanding issue for her, also related to her experience growing up with clutter. While she hated the clutter, it brought her a sense of comfort. This apparent contradiction made more sense once she completed the *Personality and Place Exercise* since she scored as an INFJ (introverted, intuitive, feeling, and judging). This means that Maribel tends to be introverted, is open to possibilities, exudes personal warmth, and likes everything in its place. So, while clutter had a familiar past-place echo, such disorder went against her grain.

Consistent with her introvertedness, Maribel likes her alone time, preferably by the beach or a soothing waterfall. She recalls going to those places in her head during times of stress. At the same time, she longed for the warmth and connectivity of family and social gatherings. So, the challenge was to help Maribel create a space that felt comfy and homey, yet organized. She loved the look of bohemian spaces and described its characteristic tchotchkes-n-things as "organized clutter." It appealed to her because it was presented in a deliberate, organized way.

Making the most of what she possessed was also important to Maribel. Her family didn't have loads of money when she was a child, but they made do. Maribel recalled their bright, colorful spaces with books and plants—something she wanted in her own space. She wanted to pass down "making do" to her children. Yet Maribel wanted to do more than draw from her family's sense of home. She also sees herself as aspiring to accomplish and be more than her family, both professionally and personally. Thus, she wanted elements that reflect her aspirational sensibilities.

Based upon all of the Design Psychology exercises I did with Maribel we came up with the following ideal statement:

> *My ideal home is a peaceful, comfortable, and loving space that is bright, uncluttered, and organized; offers a sanctuary for spiritual connection, a social space for family gatherings, encourages full creativity and cultural expression; and celebrates a strong feminine presence while welcoming a masculine one.*

The "Ideal Vision Statement" mood board Sarah created to accompany the Design Psychology Blueprint she devised for Maribel.
Credit: Mood board by Sarah-Seung MacFarland.

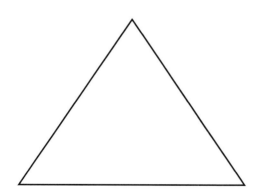

After finalizing the ideal statement and showing Maribel the *Design Psychology Blueprint* recommendations, I created mood boards to help her visualize her new space—what I'm calling her "cultural oasis."

The space is kept bright and colorful with elements of luxury, such as the velvet and gold that reflect Maribel's aspirational goals; a sense of organization as evidenced by the credenza; love of nature as symbolized by the plant and wood coffee table; and the presence of a strong Latina female presence along with a masculine one, as per the photos. I just love the Joel Meyerwitz photo of the Spanish ladies on the street! The sectional sofa, a place for Rosa and her family to relax, embodies that cozy, comfortable feel Maribel was looking for; and the chairs are additional seating for social gatherings.

"Nesting" Place Suggestions:
- Complete the *Environmental Sociogram Exercise # 6* to **ensure that, where possible, each family member has access to private, semi-private, and public space. Mothers, in particular, need to be careful not to forfeit much-needed "she-space."**
- Complete the *Personality and Place Exercise # 7* and invite other family members to complete it to **determine what kind of space layout, look, and feel supports each person's personality type.**
- Complete the *Homestyle Exercise # 8* to **identify your taste cultures past and present so that you can celebrate (not hide) that cultural heritage as expressed in your home design.**
- **If possible, consider living near or bringing your family to natural environments, so that your children can have their own transcendent experience of place.**

Lived Experience: MOVING

Finding Connection Globally and Within
by Suzan Ahmed, Ph.D.

Finding a sense of home was inevitably in my DNA. My immigrant parents, one Sudanese and one Filipina, searched for belonging in a new world—for a safe and secure place for themselves and their children. Perhaps that's why, as a psychologist/psychotherapist, I've worked with immigrants to help them to establish a sense of home, community, and connection to their inner self.

Nary, a successful, creative, Cambodian-American woman in her thirties, was one such therapy client with whom I worked. She strongly identified with her meaningful career advocating for communities of color, including, especially, immigrant and refugee communities. In our therapeutic work together, however, it became clear that Nary found it difficult to trust her inner voice amidst the expectations of her family and workplace.

Thus, a large number of our sessions focused on her ability to trust her intuitive wisdom. Toward this end, especially since her story revolved around people's search for home, I suggested incorporating Design Psychology into our therapeutic process. I hoped Design Psychology's tools could help her clarify her unique values and separate from others' expectations, all while creating a truly authentic space.

A year into her therapy, Nary also decided to move from America to Europe as she appreciated the European lifestyle and aesthetics. The fact that Nary's husband is of Dutch heritage also contributed to their eventual decision to move to the Netherlands. There she wanted to find a new home for her authentic, creative new life. I hoped our sessions would help her clarify and realize her self-home aspirations.

While the experiences of immigrants are varied and unique, themes that often show up are feeling uprooted and not "fully" feeling accepted in one culture or another because of one's family experiences, decisions, and expectations. In addition, boundary issues are common. For example, many families with traditionally collectivistic values may place less importance on personal spaces and more importance on gathering spaces. Many first- and second-generation immigrants—especially women of color—describe having these experiences.

While exploring Nary's environmental autobiography, we discovered a similar theme of diffuse boundaries. She described how family members and "unfamiliar energies" had moved in and out of her homes as she grew up. As an adult, she has rejected this dynamic. I supported her desire to create healthier boundaries with family and others, including via her strong preference for distinct "nooks."

By completing the *Ideal Home Exercise*, she arrived at a home vision that expressed her desire for balance between personal and public space:

My ideal home is a place of belonging and security. It is a sanctuary, a place of comfort, where I can be vulnerable, as well as a space where I can bring in close friends to share my passions.

Psychologist/
Psychotherapist
Suzan Ahmed, Ph.D.
Photograph by Annie Tran,
The Kindred.

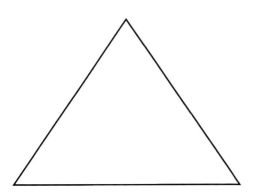

When doing the *Environmental Timeline Exercise,* Nary realized she had never previously created her own home. Instead, home was always "given to her." This awareness highlighted the importance of feeling empowered to co-create her ideal home with her husband. Central to her therapeutic process was my helping Nary envision spaces that reflected herself rather than others' expectations. For example, she described wanting more intentional items reflecting her own and others' cultures.

To help her express her whole self and passions, I encouraged her to create altar space(s) to honor her ancestors and Cambodian heritage. I suggested that she display her own and others' art. Given her love of flower arranging, I also recommended that she display her arrangements in statement vases. In addition, Nary described loving modern/contemporary design, so the idea of integrating mid-century modern pieces with European styles came to the fore.

To further support feelings of sanctuary and comfort, I suggested that she likewise integrate plants into her home. I also proposed warmer neutral colors and natural materials to soften some of the regal qualities in European architecture. Then, too, she emphasized needing more space for time alone and for her artistic and business pursuits. A private patio or garden as well as an art studio/office space including an area to make flower arrangements could contribute to meeting her needs. I also suggested creating multiple nooks throughout her home to support her introverted personality and allow her to be vulnerable.

Nary describes herself as a global citizen. Nevertheless, while she often feels connected to an expansive world, she described not always feeling that she fit into one specific box or community. She recalled her grandmother's life and home in France as a favorite home. She viewed it as an example of how to create a balance of one's own and others' cultures, integrating the "collectivistic" with a European aesthetic.

Although Nary took pride in being self-sufficient, she acknowledged that the importance of community was a value her family had instilled in her. Since feeling a sense of belonging and connection to a community was key for Nary, walkability to cafes and restaurants in her new European home became one of her priorities. Soon after supporting Nary through the process of envisioning her ideal home, she excitedly shared finding a "dream" home in an ideal Netherlands neighborhood that was central to community life and had a private patio nook and ample space for her family and creative pursuits.

In the end, given my lived experience, working with Nary and other clients whose families have immigrated to new lands resonated with me. More than ever, I too realize that what I and others want is a new kind of American Dream. It's a dream that includes the freedom to create home as a physical representation of self where we can feel secure, where our identity can be fully expressed, and where we can feel certain that we belong to both the nearby and global community.

"Moving" Space Suggestions:

- Complete the *Special Objects Inventory Exercise # 9* to **determine what possessions you want to display that give voice to your lived experience, including your culture and values as well as your unique personality and accomplishments.**
- Besides considering the interior aesthetics of your home, **choose to live in a community where you can create a balance between a sense of sanctuary and a feeling of connection to others and the wider world.**
- **When getting or giving professional design advice, ensure that such input supports the creation of home as a symbol of your actualized self**.

Lived Experience: **STANDING STRONG ALONE**

The Morgan Residence
by Toby Israel, Ph.D.[1]

Lithe, blondish, and blue-eyed like her Swedish forebears, Jennifer Morgan exudes the wonderful life force of a dancer whose creative thoughts leap always into air with glee. A children's book author, she'd survived divorce and the challenges of single parenthood. Soon to become an empty nester, Jennifer was determined to live her life *consciously*. This made her the perfect client to go through Design Psychology's awareness-raising exercises. Her conscious goal was to get recommendations for her home's new addition, a space for a woman standing strong alone.

When I first toured Jennifer's home, I could see why she wanted to renovate the modest two-family space. The side she occupied had a small, dark, narrow, living room and a nondescript kitchen. The ceilings were low with wooden beams that looked more like crude struts. It had the vibe of a struggling artist and seemed a place of paucity, not power. How could the thoughts of an inspired writer soar there?

Yet Jennifer had a model of creativity that inspired her: Barbara Morgan[2] the pre-eminent dance photographer of the twentieth century was her grandmother. Nevertheless, as the Design Psychology exercises soon revealed, Jennifer was *not* born with a silver spoon in her mouth. She had grown up in a struggling, single-parent household where her mother, a musical director, looked after Jennifer and her five siblings. Now Jennifer misses the lively hum of her brothers' and sisters' coming and going that reverberated in the hallways of her childhood. Given this family scene and her extroverted "ENTJ" personality type, Jennifer thrives on family gatherings, yet also loves looking out the window to what is beyond. At her single empty-nester crossroad, the path to more remained uncertain.

To gain more clarity about her past, present, and future lived experience, Jennifer first completed the *Environmental Family Tree Exercise*. This helped her claim her "inner farm girl". She remembered stories about her heroic Swedish early ancestors who braved brutal Minnesota winters. Their homes were farmhouses with wooden floors and bright red barns. Going through the *Guided Visualization Exercise*, she further recalled wonderful memories of times gathered around her relative's warm hearths in the Adirondack Mountains. Having completed these *past* exercises, we arrived at Jennifer's ideal home oasis vision:

> *My ideal home is organized, simple, beautiful, cozy, comfortable, and warm with flow and freedom reflecting a spirit of abundance, creativity, and vitality that comes from moving with intellectual curiosity with a community of interesting people through the heroic journey of a life where what one does counts.*

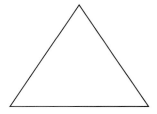

Jennifer Morgan.
Photographer unknown.

Clearly this was not a typical architectural program statement outlining the design challenge at hand. Instead, the Design Psychology process brought forth the "hidden program"[3] expressing how her new addition could support her house/oasis vision. The further exercises Jennifer completed enabled her to map her self-place path via the making of her space.

How was it translated into transcendent liberating design? Her Design Psychology Blueprint of recommendations (see Appendix) became the touchstone addressing her whole range of human needs including, especially, her lived experience past and present, and her envisioned future. She chose which memories of color, space, texture, and special objects to unpack as symbols of her best self, and which to leave behind on her road forward.

Jennifer Morgan's home with "barn" behind.
Photograph by the author.

To see what I mean, walk with me toward her remodeled home and at first you'll think the house hasn't changed. Walk closer and you'll wonder, "Is there a barn behind it?" You'll realize the "barn" is her addition *painted* the deep red of the farmhouse barns owned by her forebears. Its shape and color act as a psychological trigger reminding Jennifer that in this next empty nester stage that, "You come from ancestors with a sense of courage, of simple strength against all odds."

Open the new side-porch door and walk inside. Remembering the home's cramped interior before, you'll now feel the abundance of her new flowing dining/living room space.

There you'll see Jennifer sitting with others gathered, chatting and laughing beside a warm farmhouse stove. Take off your shoes and walk on the golden-wood floors—aged planks (like those of her other ancestors) salvaged from a long-lost Minnesota barns. As you cross the threshold, you'll step on *one* special plank reclaimed from Grandma Morgan's New York photo-studio. The plank has been reset—embedded between other floorboards. Now each time Jennifer (or you) steps on it, that plank exudes Grandma Morgan's vitality and creative powers.

Side view of Morgan's home with addition.
Photograph by the author.

Enjoy the light that fills the space from huge windows, a wall of glass. They allow Jennifer, the extrovert, to look out and be connected to, not isolated from, the world. Feel life and spirit rise as you gaze up at the room's cathedral ceiling. There, just above the mantel, is Barbara Morgan's painting entitled *Phoenix Rising*. Archetypal bird rise from the ashes and soar.

First floor plan for Jennifer Morgan's addition. (Her original living/dining, now an entry foyer, is marked in red.)
Drawing courtesy of Jennifer Morgan; Jason Kliwinski, Project Architect.

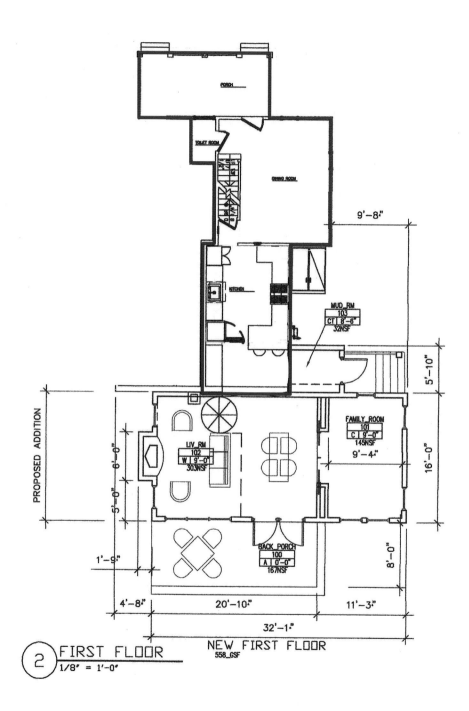

"Standing Strong Alone" Space Suggestions:
Complete the *Actualized Place Exercise # 10 to*

- ensure that your space is physically, emotionally, and financially safe and secure.
- create supportive private space for you to stand strong alone, but also space that welcomes others and is flexible should your household composition change.
- think about the lived experience of your ancestors and choose design elements that act as metaphors reminding you to celebrate any heroic aspects of their journeys and yours.
- use artwork, special objects, and other design elements that are not only beautiful but are positive triggers that inspire and uplift you.
- Combine all of these elements to create a space that feels transcendent and liberating to you.

Lived Experience: GRIEVING

The Thom Residence
by Toby Israel, Ph.D.

**Binnie Thom
and Martin Vaccaro.**
Photographer unknown.

Binnie was sixty-two when her beloved husband, Martin, died needlessly. A Vietnam vet, he was exposed to Agent Orange in his twenties. A highly toxic herbicide, Agent Orange caused the virulent form of prostate cancer that years later killed Martin, other Vietnam vets, and Vietnamese too.

After Martin died, Binnie cried everywhere to anyone about her beloved husband. Still, eventually she had to deal with many lump-in-the-throat questions like: What should I do with my husband's clothes? Should I move to a smaller house or different location? What's left for me in my life now?

The reordering of one's place and things after the death of a loved one is a metaphor for the reordering of one's life. Binnie decided to move back from Florida to New Jersey a year after Martin's funeral to surround herself with dear friends and family there.

To do so, she had to curate a whole household of possessions. Binnie busied (and distracted) herself by contemplating what things to bring and what to leave behind—a psychological as well as practical sifting. She remembered thinking:

If there are things Martin loved but I don't use, I can't be burdened with stuff. It's hard, it's painful, but things just have to go. I'll give them to charity. It's melancholy, but I'm going to get rid of things but keep those with special memories. It's not fun because it means reaching the end of my life. If I live another thirty years, I'll be lucky.

Death reminds us of our own mortality. One death reminds us of other deaths. Besides deciding which reminders of Martin to keep, Binnie realized that moving also meant disposing of special objects that belonged to her mother who had died twenty years earlier. Often guilt keeps us from throwing out, "Momma's cherished, china teacups." In Binnie's case, relinquishing things was part of the struggle of holding on to versus letting go of loved ones:

It's as if I'm throwing my mother away—cleansing, cathartic, but still painful. It was hard to clear out my mother's and father's apartment. It says, "mortality" and "finality." The person is gone all of a sudden and belongings go into Hefty trash bags.

In the end, Binnie sold almost all of her furniture and arrived at a bare, two-bedroom, New Jersey apartment she'd rented. Now she possessed only one bed, a folding chair and lots of linen, artwork, and emotions to unpack. Depressed since Martin's death, she had to force herself to get out of bed every morning. She was overwhelmed by the need to make decisions. (Martin often made the major household choices.) To help her gain control—and aid her healing process—I took Binnie through the Design Psychology exercises.

As her *Family Tree Exercise* soon revealed, Binnie grew up in an artsy, diverse, walkable community. Nevertheless, her house was painted a light gray with a gray rug since, "My mother was very bland in terms of décor. My parents had no artistic imagination. I don't feel much connection to that childhood home."

It was surprising that Binnie's childhood home was so bland since her roots were so colorful. Her mother, a former professional ballerina, grew up on a Kansas farm and was descended from Irish pseudo-gentry. Binnie's father, a charismatic, amateur actor, was the son of a Hungarian Jewish mother and a Chinese father.

Unlike her mom who gave up her career to parent, Binnie chose not to have children. She enjoyed a long career as a bilingual teacher. In fact, Binnie's fondest place memories were of times spent in Honduras, Guatemala, and Puerto Rico. Thus, when it came to envisioning her new space, rather than go toward beige or grays of her childhood home, Binnie gravitated to the lively reds, yellows, and aquas that brightened the marketplaces and festivals of her Latin America trips. Accordingly, she envisioned pale yellow in her living/dining rooms and aqua and tropical blues in her bedroom/master bath. Such a color scheme could be therapeutic, calming, and make her smile since, Binnie declared, it was, "The opposite of mourning black."

After completing further Design Psychology exercises, she devised her *Ideal Home Vision*:

> *My ideal home is near a downtown/community with activities. It is neat, compact, easy to maintain, and affordable. It is one-story with a combined living room/dining room that invites in my wide circle of family and friends yet also has a private nook for me. Light-filled, the home is comfortable, bright, lively, and colorful—an antidote to melancholy—that expresses my connections with other people, my history of accomplishments, and my warmest memories. It's the nest from which I can cope with every day.*

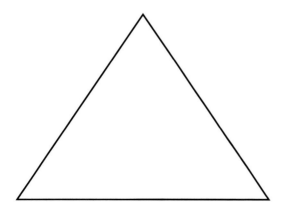

When it came to choosing furniture, although starting from scratch, Binnie's "begin again" life meant she'd jettisoned the mismatched, hand-me-down furniture she'd always owned. Instead, I helped her choose a rustic dark-wood table and cabinets that gave her living/dining room a welcoming hacienda feel.

Healing spaces often use green design elements to soothe. Yet Binnie's favorite past oasis, "that felt most sacred," was not an outdoors one. It was New York's Metropolitan Museum of Art she so often visited with her father, "that felt so grown up, open-minded and broadening. I'd just drink it in." For Binnie, strolling at her own pace past paintings was a kind of meditation that transported her "away from my issues." Thus, she preferred a space that would positively distract like "a magical [transcendent?] room that would be a virtual New York City in my own house—an always-changing wall, like in a museum."

Apropos of this (and perhaps because her dancer-mother whispered to her, too) we hung the Matisse print, *Dance (1)* on a wall by Binnie's bed. Now, every morning when she wakes, its leaping silhouettes subliminally send the message to find new joys.

To further heal from grief, she surrounded herself with jaunty weavings, ceramics, and paintings of her places she's traveled, as well as gifts from beloved friends. Still ever-present on her dresser sat her most cherished possession—a photo of Martin giving her a smooch.

It took months, but finally one day I saw her smile and heard her laugh. Soon thereafter, I snapped a photo of her looking down a hallway, staring into bright, hopeful light. I framed that image and gave it to Binnie as a present to mark the completion of her project and to serve as a visual metaphor helping her to feel that life begins again.[1]

"Grief" Space Suggestions:

- Remember that here's no right or wrong regarding ways you choose to change your environment as your life changes.
- Give yourself permission to change your home, your space, and objects in a way that best supports your well-being.
- As your life changes, consider new room uses, chose new colors and furniture, and display special objects that enable your voice to emerge.
- Grasp the opportunity to use such design psychology to envision your positive future, gain confidence in your own strengths, and grow in new, perhaps unexpected, ways.

Binnie Looking into the Light
Photograph by the author.

CHAPTER 7:
Conclusion

Life's circle comes around. As I re-read each one of these women's stories, I think of the life passages I've been through. In truth, supporting Binnie also felt cathartic for me, too. Designing her healing space helped me further heal my sense of loss of my father still lingering from so long ago. Hopefully, these self/place tales also resonate, provide insight, and, maybe, comfort you.

Still, the overarching aim of this book has been to encourage all of us to retrieve the personal, subjective sense of self and place inherent in our lives. Yet, as I hope the designing-women's stories and case studies here have shown, that sense of self, wrapped in emotional authenticity, often remains something women place-makers particularly have felt the need to hide. For most of us, in fact, the ways our self and environment are intertwined lies below the level of consciousness: it is raw, yet rich, material waiting to be mined to make ourselves and our places feel truly whole and alive!

With this in mind, my goal has been to get you *feeling* and thinking about ways you can use Design Psychology's exercises as further tools in architecture, interior design, environmental psychology, design thinking, and even art therapy to transform places, practice, and you. I hope that, in the future, others will find new ways to incorporate and expand these and other human-centered tools. The Design Psychology process provides a comprehensive methodology that can be used, not just by women place-makers, but by anyone—non-professionals or professionals of any gender identity—to create transcendent, liberating space for others and/or for one's self.

It's not easy to get minds to shift toward using lived experience as the foundation for making a place more human. Pro forma place-making practice, mindless messages from mass media, patriarchal culture, and the design critics in our heads keep us from connecting the dots between our psyches and our front doors. As often happens when a vital part of our humanity is repressed, it is women who've experienced marginalization who step forward and call for change.

The almost *all-female* American Institute of Architects' 2017 Equity, Diversity, and Inclusion Commission has used their strong voice to declare: "Architecture will go beyond physical, technical, and aesthetic distinction—it will reflect awareness and empathy. It will serve the best of humanity."[1] The architecture establishment is trying, and, in many ways, it is succeeding. "Architecture is no longer just a gentleman's profession." [2] The number of female architecture students continues to rise. The number of female deans of design schools keeps increasing. More and more women are creating spaces and public buildings in new and exciting ways.[3]

Yet what remains to be seen, as designing-women climb bravely to the top, is if they've just scaled a mountain fogged in by the same old values and practices of patriarchal clubs. Time and distance will tell if, rather than fit in, the increasing numbers of diverse professionals (and non-professionals, too) will embrace the design of exterior and interior places that result in our most fully expressed landscapes, lives, and human selves.

Sometimes culture-shifts take time. In terms of EDI, for example, the AIA admits, "We have no illusions about the scope of the challenge. Fully living up to our highest ideals and values won't happen overnight, but neither can it wait another day."[4]

In the end, to muster my own woman's voice and power, I make these final recommendations based on what I've learned about myself and from these stories of designing-women's lives.

In terms of **places**, I advise that we:

- create transcendent places that make us feel alive and tuned into our human, rather than mechanistic, experience of the world
- base such transcendent design on our lived experience in a way that gives voice to our most liberated sense of self
- ensure that the places we create honor authentic people and place connections, not just trends
- make places sensitive to life passages and life cycles in ways that support positive growth and change
- consider using metaphoric design elements, especially in our homes, that act as inspiring symbols of self—catalysts to help us achieve emotional well-being

In terms of **practice**, I advise that we:

- integrate our thinking and feeling sides and express both of these aspects of our being in our designs
- tell our own and others' personal stories in the places that we make such that design becomes a vehicle by which not only gender, but race and class identity can be expressed and celebrated, not obscured
- use our voices to challenge bias and champion empathetic, collaborative, participatory place-making processes that help overcome oppression

- elevate the interior design profession, and thereby end its disparagement throughout history due to its association with women as the "inferior other"
- ensure that design education raises students' awareness of theirs and others' stories of place and of the importance of human-centered environments and tools[5]
- explore new ways to place-make as a therapeutic technique, for example, to raise self-esteem and/or envision a positive future
- use Design Psychology's exercises to bring best memories of lived environmental experiences to the fore. By doing this, we can use those well-remembered colors, shapes, textures—sensory magic—to envision and realize our actualized places and selves

With this last point in mind, I hope you access the online Design Psychology exercises to raise your awareness of your own lived environmental experience too. I hope the exercises help you envision and write the story of *your* actualized place and self.

As for me, I had to pause when finishing this book. My mother died suddenly at almost 98. Until then she remained as sharp as any tack. For the last quarter of her life she became an actress—she'd embraced her longed-for career! When she died, I had to cancel her next gig, a one-woman show on the life of Frank Lloyd Wright. My mother died happy, fulfilled, and in an apartment with no "keep things secret" drapes or "stage-set" crystal. By then, hers was a still beautiful, but more welcoming, authentic décor.

As Gloria Steinem, herself, reflects regarding the circle of life:

But your present self also travels toward the future. That is a place not only of safety, but also of hope, dreams, and the greatest strength of your true self. If you let it, that true self will lead you. For this, you no longer need to visit rooms of the past. Instead, you will sense all the powers of nature within you.[6]

I need all of my powers now that I am orphaned. What should I do next? I've just welcomed my first grandchild—a girl! I hope her parents don't mind, I plan to help her dig in dirt, watch worms squirm, and delight in blue jays. As she grows up and learns to fly, I'll cheer her on, saying, "The best person to design a woman's life is each glorious woman herself."

Appendix

Jennifer Morgan's Ideal Home Blueprint

My ideal home is organized, simple, beautiful, cozy, comfortable, and warm with flow and freedom reflecting a spirit of abundance, creativity, and vitality that comes from moving with intellectual curiosity with a community of interesting people through the heroic journey of a life where what one does counts.

Growth

- Ensure that alterations to your home maximize the number units to provide income while retaining (or increasing) the resale value of your home.
- Ensure that any alterations provide flexibility so that your home can be adapted depending upon life-changes in the upcoming years including change in family size/composition and aging.
- Ensure that any alterations address a lifestyle that could include six months in residence elsewhere.
- Where possible, install environmental-friendly heating, cooling, etc., systems that are reasonably cost-effective in the short and long term.
- Consider ways your home might be further adapted as a place for future projects/your community.

Look And Feel

- Ensure that both the exterior and interior of the home retains an old "farmish"/rustic feeling that also acknowledges your European, French country, castle heritage.
- Ensure that any alteration to your home maximize its setting on a large lot including via views creating a sense of connection to the backyard/outdoors.
- Increase the amount of planting on all sides of your yard/driveway to create a visual barrier between your yard and your neighbors' yards.
- Create an improved, welcoming, beautiful entry.
- Consider planting fruit-bearing trees at the rear of your backyard.
- Consider installing new shutters on the exterior of your house.
- Create a look and feel within your home that balances simplicity and orderliness with a feeling of creativity and vitality.
- Use natural materials including wood and stone.
- Use artwork, books, and other special objects.
- Where possible, repeat molding features around doorways throughout the house.
- Where possible, increase the amount of light throughout the house including via large windows, glass doors, and/or skylights.
- Decorate your home using a combination of vibrant colors and more subdued "monastery-like" colors, i.e., peacock blue in your study; grayish/tan in your living room.
- If possible, raise the roof of any great room and expose and/or create wood-beamed ceilings.
- Install a masonry stove or fireplace at the core of the house.

Layout

- Consider creating a circular driveway and separate front entrance to your home for use exclusively by tenants.
- Consider creating a new front entrance on the side of your house including a monastery-like courtyard and carport/turnaround.
- Consider creating an internal courtyard/outdoor "room" in your backyard adjacent to your house
- Consider creating a further area in your backyard to include a goldfish pond or other water feature.
- Consider creating the majority of your personal living space on the ground floor via the addition of a great room/extension and garage conversion to include an office and master bedroom/bath.
- In creating additional rooms/space balance a sense of abundant space while retaining cozy areas that make you feel embraced.
- Retain a sense of flow between areas while retaining separation from renters.
- Create a living room spacious enough to accommodate dancing, singing, and a piano.
- Create an office space that enables you to face the outdoors and initially allow for two desks, i.e., one for you and one for your son.
- Consider creating a gallery hallway connection from the main house to the renovated garage
- Create at least one other rentable room.
- Ensure that any reconfiguration of rooms also includes a guest bedroom space.
- Consider creating a second laundry room, possibly on the ground floor.

Objects and furniture

- Include beautiful, precious objects (but not too many) around your house and place them with intentionality to help create a spiritual space.
- Place your grandmother's painting in a central, prominent place.
- Place Dana's painting in a central, prominent place.
- Consider blowing up and mounting other key photos by your grandmother and placing them in a prominent place.
- Select portions of your grandfather's typeface and place them prominently in the house.
- Place other photos of family and friends in a prominent place.
- Place books around your house including display of the books you've written.
- Place artwork around the house including the work of your book illustrator.
- Place your "box with leaves" in a prominent place.
- Have your sister create a beautiful Adirondack-type bench(es) for your home to be placed under a window or possibly as part of your dining room set.
- Consider the inclusion of a beautiful water sculpture outside your house.
- Include a birdfeeder in your backyard.

Binnie Thom's Ideal Home Blueprint

My ideal home is near a downtown/community with activities. It is neat, compact, easy to maintain, and affordable. It is one-story with a combined living room/dining room that invites in my wide circle of family and friends yet also has a private nook for me. Light-filled, the home is comfortable, bright, lively, and colorful—an antidote to melancholy—that expresses my connections with other people, my history of accomplishments, and my warmest memories. It's the nest from which I get to cope with every day.

Growth

- Decorate your current home in a way that considers that you might move in the future.
- If you do move, consider living in a walkable town/small city where there are lots of activities.
- Choose a home that requires low maintenance, thereby freeing you from any worry about upkeep.
- Particularly, choose and create a home that supports your transitions between coupledom and singlehood, nurturing your confidence in your ability to live a full and happy life on your own or with a future partner.

Look And Feel

- Create a home with a look and feel that reflects your sensing personality type that's streamlined and without frills.
- Ensure that your house is light-filled and includes views of trees/nature.
- Choose décor for your home to express your quasi-folk culture that's different from your parent's lower middle décor and your Tampa home's formal feel since you felt no attachment to either of those decors.
- Particularly express your "self" and your ethnic attachments including to Latino culture and your experiences in Honduras, Guatemala, Columbia, and Spain by creating a fun, home space of bright colors, weavings, etc., that reflect the *joi-de-vivre* of Latino culture, language, and festivities.
- For example, consider a color scheme of warm, bright red-orange, gold, and blue (like Mexican plate decor) and Marimeko type colorful fabrics—the opposite of your parent's home's bland light gray.
- While your public space is fun and colorful, consider decorating your bedroom in more calming water-like blues.
- Consider ways to decorate your private sunroom that would make it "magical" yet relaxing for you, for instance, as in a "virtual NYC" with an always-changing wall or museum-like atmosphere that is diverse, interesting, challenging, fun, and active.
- Place your CD player in easy reach to daily turn on music that soothes-calms-uplifts you.

Layout

Choose a home that is not too big and formal.

- For example, a home with two bedrooms, two baths, a space for a desk (although not necessarily a study), and an open living room for small gatherings.
- Design the kitchen space as a place not only to cook and eat, but to spend private time.
- Also create a private space like your current sunroom that acts as an oasis just for you to watch TV, crochet, meditate, relax, or even sleep.

Objects and furniture

- Use the opportunity of creating your new home to jettison any hand-me-down furniture and instead select furniture that not only meets your practical needs but makes the house feel your own.
- Retain furniture that you really like or that has meaning for you like your great grandfather's desk and end tables that Martin refinished.
- Place objects around your home that have meaning to you and tell a story, like self-made items, gifts from friends and family, scrapbooks, souvenirs, Greta's prints and weavings, your mother's pillows, needlepoint from Martin's mother, your purple vase, your afghan, and your teacher-retirement blanket. Don't use things just to "accessorize."
- Chose items that remind you of the best of your past while also including items that symbolize the best of your future yet to come.
- For example, continue to display your favorite photos of you and Martin and keep certain artwork, glassware, and jewelry that Martin made or things you bought together. Give away other things that Martin loved if you think they might burden you physically and/or emotionally.
- Beyond this, also display mementoes of your activities, past accomplishments, and *new* pieces such as Matisse's painting of dancers, and photos of the family and friends that love and support you now.
- Camouflage your current desk/electronic equipment/workspace area via storage cabinets, curtains, the use of fabrics, and other design interventions to ensure that the "burden of paperwork" isn't always present.
- Consider placing colorful fabric on top of your apartment's current vertical blinds to help make the space bright and lively while also allowing light to filter in.
- Add big plants all around your house including, especially, low-maintenance plants.
- Include in your sunroom a new ideal chair(s) like your cousin's ergonomic one that reclines.
- Include a new reading light in the sunroom that enables you to read and crochet there comfortably.
- Also consider adding a fountain that creates a calming effect, perhaps in the sunroom.

Endnotes

Endnotes

Introduction

1. Toby Israel, *Some Place Like Home: Using Design Psychology to Create Ideal Places* (Chichester: Wiley/Academy Editions, 2003).

2. Mary Field Belenky, Blythe McVicker Clinchy, Nancy Rule Goldberger, and Jill Mattuck Tarule, *Women's Ways of Knowing: The Development of Self, Voice, and Mind* (New York: Basic Books, 1986).

3. As described in Israel, *Some Place Like Home*, I took male design notables Michael Graves, Charles Jencks, and Andes Duany through my Design Psychology exercises.

4. Elena Ferrante, "Power Is a Story Told by Women," *The New York Times*, May 19, 2019.

CHAPTER 1:
Designing Women's Lives
Draperies, My Mother, and Me

1. Pat Kirkham, ed., *Women Designers in the USA 1900-2000: Diversity and Difference* (New York: Yale University Press, 2000), 305.

2. "Sister Parish," Wikipedia, accessed November 27, 2021, https://en-academic.com/dic.nsf/enwiki/59534.

3. "Sister Parish."

Herstory of Place-making

1. John Pile, *A History of Interior Design* (Hoboken: John Wiley & Sons, 2005), 301.

2. Pile, *Interior Design*, 301.

3. Allison Carll White, "What's in a Name? Interior Design and/or Interior Architecture: The Discussion Continues," *Journal of Interior Design* 35, no 1 (May 2009).

4. Kirkham, *Women Designers*, 305.

5. Tina Gianoulis and Claude J. Summers, "Interior Design," GLBTQ, accessed 2015, http://www.glbtq.com.

6. Pile, *Interior Design*, 269.

7. Pile, 310.

8. Elsie de Wolfe," Wikipedia, accessed November 24, 2021, https://en.wikipedia.org/wiki/Elsie_de_Wolfe.

9. Wikipedia, "Coverture," accessed December 13, 2021, https://en.wikipedia.org/wiki/Coverture.

10. Libby Sellers, *Women Design* (New York: Frances Lincoln, 2017), 45.

11. Sellers, *Women Design*, 46.

12. Sellers, 46.

13. Kirkham, *Women Designers* 305.

14. Kirkham, 305.

15. Lucinda Havenhand, "A View from the Margin: Interior Design," *Design Issues* 20, no. 4 (September 2004): 33.

16. Havenhand, "View from the Margin," 33.

17. Kirkham, 305.

18. Despina Stratigakos, *Where Are the Women Architects?* (Princeton: Princeton University Press, 2016), 7.

19. Diane Favro, "Sincere and Good: The Architectural Practice of Julia Morgan," in "Women's Voices in Architecture and Planning," special issue, *Journal of Architectural and Planning Research* 9, no. 2 (Summer, 1992): 116.

20. "LGBTQ Interior Designers," Queerbio.com, accessed Feb. 21, 2020, http://queerbio.com/wiki/index.php/LGBTQ_Interior_Designers

21. Elizabeth Borneman, "Study Suggests that Men Aren't Better at Reading Maps Than Women," October 1, 2016, accessed Dec. 13, 2021, https://www.geographyrealm.com/study-suggests-men-arent-better-reading-maps-women/.

22. Sally Ann Drucker, "Betty Friedan: The Three Waves of Feminism," *Ohio Humanities Blog and News*, April 27, 2018.

23. Betty Friedan, *The Feminine Mystique* (New York: W.W. Norton & Company, 1963).

24. Friedan, *Feminine Mystique*, 57.

25. Gina Rippon, *Gender and Our Brain: How New Neuroscience Explodes the Myth of the Female Brains* (New York: Pantheon Books, 2019).

26. Rippon, *Gender and Our Brain*, 3.

27. Daniel Goleman, *Emotional Intelligence* (New York: Bantam Books, 1995).

28. Goleman, *Emotional Intelligence*, 131.

29. Goleman, 131.

30. Goleman, 131.

31. Rippon, 54.

32. Andrew Reiner, *Better Boys, Better Men: The New Masculinity That Creates Greater Courage and Emotional Resiliency* (San Francisco: Harper One, 2020).

33. Reiner, *Better Boys*, 32.

34. Reiner, 70

35. Karen Franck, "A Feminist Approach to Architecture: Acknowledging Women's Way of Knowing," in *Architects: A Place for Women*, ed. Ellen Perry Berkeley, Ellen Perry, and Matilda McQuaid (Washington: The Smithsonian Institution Press, 1989).

36. Franck, "Feminist Approach," 201.

37. Franck, 202.

38. Franck, 202.

39. Franck, 203. Of course, I am simplifying these thinkers' insights. In fact, Franck herself offers seven feminist ways of knowing. Her insightful article elaborates by identifying seven qualities that characterize feminine or feminist ways of knowing and analyzing.

40. Franck, 201.

41. Griselda Pollock, quoted in Sherry Ahrentzen, "The 'F' Word in Architecture," in *Reconstructing Architecture Critical Discourses and Social Practices*, ed. Thomas A. Dutton and Lian Hurst Mann (Minneapolis: University of Minnesota Press, 1996), 99.

42. Clarissa Pinkola Estes, *Women Who Run with Wolves: Myths and Stories of the Wild Woman Archetype* (Rivcr Wolfe Press, 2017) Kindle, Introduction.

Julia Morgan, AIA

1. "Gold Medal," American Institute of Architects, accessed October 13, 2021, https://www.aia.org/awards/7046-gold-medal

2. Favro, "Sincere and Good," 125.

3. Mark Anthony Wilson, *Julia Morgan: Architect of Beauty* (Salt Lake: Gibbs Smith, 2007), 6.

4. Russell L. Quacchia, *Julia Morgan Architect and the Creation of the Asilomar Conference Grounds* (USA: Russell L. Quacchia, 2005), 103.

5. Favro, 116.

6. Favro, 115

7. Favro, 116

8. Favro, 113.

9. Favro, 123.

10. Favro, 123.

11. Quacchia, *Julia Morgan*, 173.

12. Wilson, *Julia Morgan*, 200–201.

13. Karen McNeill, "Julia Morgan: Gender, Architecture, and Professional Style," *Pacific Historical Review* 76, no. 2 (May 2007): 267.

14. Favro, 124.

15. Wilson, 19.

16. Wilson, 17.

17. Favro, 117.

18. Favro, 117.

19. Favro, 113.

20. Favro, 117.

21. Favro, 125.

22. Wilson, 200.

CHAPTER 2:
The Heroine's Journey
Woman's Search for Meaning

1. Project Unicorn, based at the McKnight School in East Windsor, N.J. was funded by the National Endowment for the Arts.

2. Elizabeth (Betsy) Caesar. See The Play and Playground Encyclopedia, "Betsy Caesar," https://www.pgpedia.com/c/betsy-caesar.

3. Diane K. Osbon, ed., *Reflections on the Art of Living: A Joseph Campbell Companion* (New York: Harper Collins Publishers, Inc., 1991), 181.

4. Edith Cobb, *The Ecology of the Imagination in Childhood* (New York: Columbia University Press, 1977) 54–55.

5. Cobb, *Ecology*, 54–55.

6. Clare Cooper Marcus, "The House as a Symbol of Self," in *Environmental Psychology: People and their Physical Settings*, ed. H. Proshansky, W. Ittelson, and L. Rivlin (New York: Holt, Rinehart and Winston, 1976), 435–448.

7. Christopher Jones, former Dean of Faculty and Head of School of Architecture at Hull University was the person who stood up for me.

Finding Your Woman's Voice

1. *Joseph Campbell and the Power of Myth*, with Bill Moyers. (St. Paul, MN: High Bridge, 1988), audiotape.

2. Joseph Campbell, *The Hero With a Thousand Faces* (New York: Bollingen Foundation, 1949).

3. Will Linn, "Joseph Campbell is the Hidden Link Between '2001,' 'Star Wars,' and 'Mad Max: Fury Road,'" *IndieWire*, March 12, 2018, accessed November 27, 2021, https://www.indiewire.com/2018/03/joseph-campbell-heros-journey-2001-star-wars-1201937470/.

4. Joseph Campbell, *Pathways to Bliss:*

Mythology and Personal Transformation (Novato, CA: New World Library, 2004), 119.

5. Maureen Murdock, *The Heroine's Journey* (Boston: Shambhala Publications, Inc., 1990).

6. Murdock, *Heroine's Journey*, 3.

7. Maureen Murdock, *The Heroine's Journey* (Boston: Shambhala Publications, Inc., 2013), Preface to the eBook Edition, Kindle.

8. Murdock, *Heroine's Journey*, Preface, Kindle.

9. Murdock, *Heroine's Journey*, 3.

10. Murdock, *Heroine's Journey*, Preface, Kindle.

11. Murdock, *Heroine's Journey*, 88.

12. Murdock, *Heroine's Journey*, Preface, Kindle.

13. Belenky et al., *Women's Ways of Knowing*.

14. Belenky et al.

15. Belenky et al., 69.

16. Belenky et al., 144.

17. Belenky et al., 141.

18. Franck, "Feminist Approach."

19. Franck, 203.

20. Franck, 210.

21. Belenky et al., 103.

22. Israel, *Some Place Like Home*, 197.

23. Israel, 197–198.

Margo Grant Walsh

1. Sam Perkins, "Silent Masters: Margo Grant Walsh 1936 – Present," accessed September 28, 2021, https://silentmasters.net/article/margo-grant/.

2. Griselda Pollock, *Vision and Difference*, quoted in Ahrentzen, "The 'F' Word," 99.

3. I conducted three sessions with Margo Grant Walsh to take her through my Design Psychology Toolbox of exercises. The first two sessions occurred in 2001. The third session occurred in 2015. She provided me with further information regarding her life and work in a series of emails in August 6, 2020 to January 16, 2020. This section is based on the information thus obtained from her.

4. Marilyn Loden, *Feminine Leadership or How to Succeed at Business Without Being One of the Boys* (New York: Times Books, 1985), 26, 63.

5. The questionnaire I administered to Margo Grant Walsh was loosely based on personality types identified by Carl Gustav Jung that were later used as the jumping off point for the Myers-Briggs Type Indicator. For more on the questionnaire, see David Keirsey and Marilyn Bates, *Please Understand Me: Character &Temperament Types* (Del Mar, CA.: Gnosology Books, Ltd., 1984).

6. Perkins comments, "Their appeal may say something about the collector herself. They are humble, sturdy, easily transported and adaptable to multiple uses." Perkins, "Silent Masters."

7. Anthony Iannacci, ed., *Developing the Architecture of the Workplace: Gensler 1967-1997* (New York: Edizioni Press, Inc., 1998).

8. Timothy A. O'Brien with Margo Grant Walsh, *Collecting by Design: Silver and Metalwork of the Twentieth Century from the Margo Grant Walsh Collection* (Houston: The Museum of Fine Arts, 2008).

9. Nancy McClure, "Adornment of the American West: The American Indian as Artist," Buffalo Bill Center, June 10, 2015, accessed September 28, 2021, https://centerofthewest.org/2015/06/ Perkins, opt.cit. 10/adornment-in-the-west-the-american-indian-as-artist/.

CHAPTER 3:
Women on Fire
Igniting Design Psychology

1. Abrahma Maslow, *Motivation and Personality* (New York: Harper and Row, 1954), 163.

2. All of the original Design Psychology Toolbox of exercises can be accessed via http://www.designpsychology.net/pdf/Some-Place-Like-Home-Excercises.pdf.

3. See Toby Israel, *Some Place Like Home*, 209, for more about these Design Psychology Steps and the Design Psychology Toolbox of exercises.

4. Katja Battarbee, Jane Fulton Suri, and Suzanne Gibbs Howard, "Empathy on the Edge," (IDEO Brown, 2009), 2.

5. For more on IDEO, see https://www.ideo.com/.

6. Nina Azzarello, "Interview with Jane Fulton Suri," *DesignBoom*, April 25, 2016, accessed August 2020, https://www.designboom.com/design/jane-fulton-suri-interview-ideo-little-book-of-design-research-ethics-04-25-2016/

7. Jane Fulton Suri, personal correspondence with author, October 23, 2020.

8. Jon Kolko, *Thoughts on Interaction Design* (Savannah: Brown Bear, 2007), 11.

16. *"Student Wellbeing,"* The Green School, accessed November 30, 2021, https://www.greenschool.org/bali/student-wellbeing/

17. *"Student Wellbeing."*

18. Hardy was born in Canada.

19. Claire Turrell, "How a former DKNY designer launched an architecture firm in Bali that builds modern, million-dollar jungle mansions out of bamboo," Insider, June 14, 2021, https://www.insider.com/bamboo-mansions-bali-photos-elora-hardy-ibuku-feature-2021-6.

20. Turrell, "Former DKNY designer."

21. Turrell.

22. The placard near the Oculus explains: *"On 9/11 each year, weather permitting, the skylight of the Oculus will be opened to allow the sun to fill this entire space. Envisioned by* Santiago Calatrava *to symbolize a dove released from a child's hand, the Oculus is situated at an angle in contrast to neighboring buildings and even the entire grid of the city, thereby allowing the light to shine directly overhead and for the sun to move across its axis exactly on September 11th each year."* Eric Baldwin, *"World Trade Center Transportation Hub Oculus Designed in Remembrance of 9/11," ArchDaily, September 11, 2008,* https://www.archdaily.com/901840/world-trade-center-transportation-hub-oculus-designed-in-remembrance-of-9-11.

23. Sparke, *As Long As It's Pink*, 231.

24. Denise Scott Brown, *Having Words* (London: Architectural Association, 2009), 114–115.

25. David Brett, *C. R. Mackintosh: The Poetics of Workmanship* (London: Reaktion Books Ltd., 1992), 27.

26. Timothy Neat, "Tinker, Tailor, Soldier, Sailor: Margaret Macdonald and the Principle of Choice," in *Glasgow Girls' Women in Art and Design 1880–1920*, ed. Jude Burkhauser (Edinburgh: Cannongate Publishing Limited, 1990), 117.

27. Timothy Neat, *Part Seen, Part Imagined: Meaning and Symbolism in the Work of Charles Rennie Mackintosh and Margaret Macdonald* (Edinburgh: Canongate Press, 1994), 13.

28. Thomas Howarth, Charles Rennie Mackintosh, 1868-1928 : a memorial exhibition catalogue (Toronto: Art Gallery of Ontario, 1978).

29. Janice Helland, *The Studios of Frances and Margaret Macdonald* (Manchester: Manchester University Press, 1996), 73.

30. Helland, *Studios*, 157.

31. Helland, 174.

32. Neat, *Part Seen*, 21.

33. Judith Kinchin, Liz Bird, and Thomas Howarth, "Second City of the Empire,'" in *Glasgow Girls' Women in Art and Design 1880–1920*, ed. Jude Burkhauser (Edinburgh: Cannongate Publishing Limited, 1990), 34.

34. Brett, *C. R. Mackintosh*, 110.

35. Brett, 116.

36. Neat, *Part Seen*, 16.

37. Neat, *Part Seen*, 21.

38. Alexander, *Book One*, 40–41.

39. Helland, 132.

40. Neat, "Tinker, Tailor," 81–106.

41. Neat, "Tinker, Tailor," 102–103.

42. Helland, 132.

43. Brett, 130.

44. Brett, 130.

45. The Mackintoshes' home at 78 Southpark Avenue (originally 6 Florentine Terrace) where they lived from 1906 to 1914 has been reconstructed in the Hunterian Art Gallery in Glasgow.

46. Comment by a visitor to the Mackintosh home, now part of the exhibit at the Hunterian Gallery.

Liberating Design

1. Leilah Stone, "In Defense of Decoration," Metropolis, Sept. 22, 2020, https://metropolismag.com/viewpoints/in-defense-of-decoration/.

2. Lesley-Ann Noel, "My manifesto toward changing the conversation around race, equity and bias in design," Future of Design in Higher Education, July 3, 2020, https://medium.com/future-of-design-in-higher-education/9-steps-towards-changing-the-conversation-around-race-equity-and-bias-in-design-304242194116.

3. Noel, "Manifesto."

4. Paulo Freire, *Pedagogy of the Oppressed* (New York: Continuum, 1970).

5. Freire, *Pedagogy*, 77.

6. This is a translation of the Portuguese word, "conscientizacao," that Freire used.

7. Freire, 12.

8.   "The BADG Manifesto," Black Artists + Designers Guild, accessed December 1, 2021. https://www.badguild.info/badg-manifesto.

9.   "The BADG Manifesto."

10. In collaboration with architects Leyden Lewis and Nin Cooke John.

11. Leilah Stone, "A Virtual Home Imagines a More Free and Authentic Future for Black Families," Metropolis, February 19, 2021, https://metropolismag.com/projects/obsidian-virtual-concept-house-badg/.

12. Stone, "Virtual Home."

13. Stone, "Virtual Home."

14. Stone, "Virtual Home."

15. Stone, "Virtual Home."

16. Stone, "Virtual Home."

17. "About Malene Barnett," accessed November 21, 2021, https://malenebarnett.com/about

18. "About Malene Barnett."

Gloria Steinem

1.   Place-making professionals who are members of the following professional organizations typically use that group's initials after their name: American Institute of Architects (AIA); Fellow of the American Institute of Architects (FAIA); American Society of Interior Designers (ASID); International Interior Design Association (IIDA).

2.   Gloria Steinem, *Revolution from Within: A Book of Self-Esteem* (New York: Little, Brown and Company, 1992).

3.   Hooks, *All About Love*, 60.

4.   Steinem, *Revolution*, 7.

5.   Gloria Steinem, *My Life on the Road* (New York: Random House, 2015), 249.

6.   Cooper Marcus, "House as a Symbol of Self."

7.   Gloria Steinem, *Revolution from Within: A Book of Self-Esteem* (Kindle Edition), chap. 1, sec. 3, Kindle.

8.   Gloria Steinem, "A Personal Preface," in *Revolution from Within: A Book of Self-Esteem*, Kindle.

9.   Nancy J. Napier, *Recreating Your Self: Building Self-Esteem Through Imaging and Self-Hypnosis* (New York: Norton, 1990).

10. Steinem, *Revolution*, chap. 4, sec. 2, Kindle.

11. Steinem, *Revolution*, 141–142.

12. Steinem, *Revolution*, chap. 7, sec. 1, Kindle.

13. Steinem, *Revolution*, chap. 7, sec. 1, Kindle.

14. Gerald and Lindsay Zaltman, *Marketing Metaphoria: What Deep Metaphors Reveal about the Minds of Consumers* (Boston: Harvard Business Press, 2008), Chapter 4, Kindle.

15. Israel, *Some Place Like Home*, 6.

16. Steinem, *Revolution*, chap. 4, sec. VII, Kindle.

17. Steinem, *Revolution*, 173.

18. Steinem, *Revolution*, chap. 4, sec. VII, Kindle.

19. Steinem, *Revolution*, 19.

20. "How Gloria Steinem Is Using Her Home To Create A Safe Space For Women," The Breakfast Club, accessed December 30, 2021, https://thebreakfastclub.iheart.com/featured/breakfast-club/content/2020-11-04-how-gloria-steinem-is-using-her-home-to-create-a-safe-space-for-women/.

21. Steinem, *Revolution*, chap.5, sec. 1, Kindle.

22. "How Gloria Steinem Is Using Her Home To Create A Safe Space For Women."

23. Steinem, *My Life on the Road*, 250.

24. "Gloria's Foundation," accessed November 30, 2021, https://www.gloriasfoundation.org/

25. "A Home for a Movement," Gloria's Foundation, accessed November 30, 2021, https://artsandculture.google.com/story/a-home-for-a-movement/jgIi1197UxiDIA

26. Bella Abzug (1920–1998) was a social activist, leader of the women's movement and U.S. congresswoman. Dorothy Pitman Hughes (1938-) is an activist and a leading New York City battered-women and child-welfare advocate.

27. Steinem, *My Life on the Road*, 250.

28. "How Gloria Steincm Is Using IIer IIome To Create A Safe Space For Women."

29. Steinem, *My Life on the Road*, 251.

30. Steinem, *Revolution*, chap 4, sec. 2, Kindle.

CHAPTER 5
Healing by Design Psychology
The Road to Wellness

1. This section is an edited version of this blog post: Israel, "The Road to Wellness: A Journey via Design Psychology," Design on My Mind, Psychology Today, October 31, 2011, https://www.psychologytoday.com/us/node/77969/preview.

2. Anndee Hochman, "Inner Realms," Philadelphia Enquirer, January 5, 2007.

3. See: https://www.ywcaprinceton.org/about/

4. See: "Healing Design Presentations," Oasis By Design, http://www.oasisbydesign.net/presentation.html

5. See Israel, "Design Psychology Exercises," accessible at: http://www.designpsychology.net/pdf/Some-Place-Like-Home-Excercises.pdf.

6. See: http://www.designpsychology.net/pdf/Some-Place-Like-Home-Excercises.pdf.

7. The late Laura Martin was the Education Director at BCRC

8. Kara Stephenson was the Director at BCRC.

9. Also see: Clare Cooper Marcus and Marni Barnes, *Healing Gardens: Therapeutic Benefits and Design Recommendations* (New York: Wiley, 1999).

10. I ran focus groups for Northern Westchester Hospital in Mt. Kisco, N.Y. This resulted in recommendations for the Ken Hamilton Caregiver Center that was established there. See: "Ken Hamilton Caregivers Center," Northern Westchester Hospital, https://nwh.northwell.edu/your-visit/ken-hamilton-caregivers-center.

11. A landmark study by Roger Ulrich (1984) found that patients with views of nature used less narcotic and milder analgesics, indicating lower pain experience. Such patients also had shorter hospital stays and a more positive surgical recovery overall than those whose views included no natural elements.

The "Neuros," Women, and Metaphoria

1. For more on the Academy for Neuroscience in Architecture, see: https://anfarch.ucsd.edu/HomePage.

2. Millicent Gappell, "Psychoneuroimmunology," in *Innovations in Healthcare Design*, ed. S. Marberry (New York: Van Nostrand Reinhold, 1995), 116.

3. For further discussion, see Toby Israel, "Oasis by Design Psychology," *The Nurture Report* 3, no. 3 (December, 2009).

4. Esther M. Sternberg, *Healing Spaces: The Science of Place and Well-Being* (Cambridge and London: The Belknap Press of Harvard University Press, 2009), 102.

5. Belleruth Naparstek, *Invisible Heroes: Survivors of Trauma and How They Heal* (New York: Bantam Books, 2006), 150.

6. Naparstek, *Invisible Heroes*, 150.

7. Naparstek, 150.

8. Jill Pable, "Interior Design Identity in the Crossfire: A Call for Renewed Balance in Subjective and Objective Ways of Knowing," *Journal of Interior Design* 34, no. 2 (2009): viii.

9. Pable, "Interior Design," ix.

10. Pable, viii.

11. Pable, xiii

12. Pable.

13. Pable, xvi.

14. Lucinda Kaukas Havenhand, "A Re-View from the Margin: Interior Design," *Design Issues* 35, no. 1 (Winter 2019): 71.

15. Havenhand, "Re-View," 72.

16. Rippon, 91.

17. Juhani Pallasmaa, *The Thinking Hand* (Chichester: John Wiley, 2009), 118–119.

18. Zaltman and Zaltman, *Marketing Metaphoria*.

19. Zaltman and Zaltman, 13.

20. Zaltman and Zaltman, xviii.

21. Zaltman and Zaltman, 19.

22. Zaltman and Zaltman, 98.

23. Zaltman and Zaltman, 81.

24. Zaltman and Zaltman, xviii.

25. Zaltman and Zaltman, 63-64. Also see Chapter 4: Transformation, 63–80.

26. Zaltman and Zaltman, 64.

27. Zaltman and Zaltman, 64.

28. Rubin Battino, *Metaphoria: Metaphor and Guided Metaphor for Psychotherapy and Healing* (Norwalk, CT: Crown House Publishing Ltd., 2005).

29. Battino's work was inspired by a 'brief therapy' method utilizing storytelling, pioneered by renowned therapist Milton H. Erickson. Belleruth Naparstek and Gloria Steinem's therapist, Nancy Napier was also influenced by Erickson's approach. For more, see "The Milton H. Erickson Foundation," https://www.erickson-foundation.org/.

30. Battino, *Metaphoria*, xiii.

31. Battino, 155.

32. Battino, 100.

33. Battino, 103.

34. Battino, xiii.

35. Battino, xii – xiii.

36. Battino

37. Battino, 294.

38. Battino, 294.

39. Battino, 279.

40. Battino, 278.

41. From Anthology "Definition Wallpapers," Harlequin/Sanderson Design Group, https://harlequin.sandersondesigngroup.com/collections/anthology-definition-wallpapers/

42. Osborn, 185.

43. Sophie Louise Draper interview, Harlequin Sanderson Design Group, 2017.

Esther Sternberg, MD

1. Esther M. Sternberg, *The Balance Within: The Science Connecting Health and Emotions* (New York: W. H. Freeman and Company, 2001).

2. Sternberg, *Healing Spaces*.

3. Sternberg, *Healing Spaces*, 148.

4. I met with Sternberg on November 15, 2010, in Las Vegas, where she presented to the Healthcare Design.10 Conference.

5. Esther M. Sternberg, *The Science of Healing: Understanding the Mind/Body Connection with Dr. Esther Sternberg* (PBS, 2010), DVD.

6. Sternberg, *The Balance Within*, xv.

7. Some years after our meeting, Sternberg left her position at the National Institute of Mental Health in Bethesda, Maryland, to become Research Director for the Andrew Weil Center for Integrative Medicine and the Founding Director of the Institute on Place, Wellbeing and Performance at the University of Arizona, Tucson.

CHAPTER 6
Women Make Space

1. See the "Keirsey Temperament Sorter" in David Keirsey and Marilyn Bates, *Please Understand Me: Character, Temperament and Types* (Del Mar, CA: Gnostic, 1984).

2. The name "Katya" is used as a pseudonym as "Katya" wished to remain anonymous.

3. According to Katya, "Building biology is a field of building science that investigates indoor living and work environments for a variety of health hazards. In particular, it looks at how the environment of your home or workspace can affect your health, creating either restful or stressful places for you to spend time in. As a building biologist, my main job is to assess/identify indoor pollutants (potential health hazards) and identify their sources in the environment, and then suggest solutions to help avoid or minimize occupant exposure to these potential health hazards. The assessments vary from measuring occupant exposure to electromagnetic fields and radiation (from internal and external sources), assessing the home for moisture and mold issues and other allergens and/or volatile organic compounds. It also involves advising clients on healthier cleaning and personal care product alternatives as well as healthy bedding and building materials." Email communication with author, May 19, 2021.

One Woman's Journey from Oppression to Self-Realization

1. As Katya explains, "The Medicine Wheel is the Sacred Circle of Life, a cosmology followed by native tribes around the globe. It signifies the meeting place between heaven and earth. It represents totality of all life; the beginning and the end, the cycles of the universe, of life, of the seasons, of the day, of the moon and of bringing an idea to fruition. It is a holistic model for living. Medicine in this context is viewed as anything that helps you to achieve a greater connection to Spirit and the natural world around you. Using a Medicine Wheel in your home can deepen your connection to the cycles of nature and can bring a natural perspective to your view of life." Email communication with author, May 19, 2021.

2. The *Special Objects Inventory* exercise was included in Israel, *Some Place Like Home*, adapted with permission from Clare Cooper Marcus, *House as Mirror of Self: Exploring the Deeper Meaning of Home* (Newburyport, MA: Nicolas-Hays, Inc, 2006), 79.

3. Three years later, Katya wrote to me: "As I am writing this, my partner and I have just embarked on a new chapter in our lives. We are planning our wedding and are looking to buy our first family home. We are looking for a similar style house in a neighborhood by the beach to create our simple, cozy, nurturing sanctuary for our own little family." Email communication with author.

Transformation by Design

1. In *Some Place Like Home*, I also adapted the original Design Psychology Toolbox for use with groups, not just individuals.

2. Israel, *Some Place Like Home*.

Becoming

1. Israel, *Some Place Like Home.*
2. Cooper Marcus, *House as Mirror of Self.*

Standing Strong Alone

1. This section is an edited version of the blog post: Israel, "Women By Design: Transforming Home, Transforming Self, Part I: The Three Muses," Design on My Mind, Psychology Today, July 2, 2015, https://www.psychologytoday.com/us/node/1076830/preview.

2. Barbara Morgan (1900–1992) was widely known for her photographs of dancers, including the photograph of Martha Graham in her swirling skirt.

3. The term 'architecture program' refers to the research and decision-making process that identifies the scope of work involved in a project's design. It is the typical first step before the design process begins. Yet, commenting on the "hidden program," Ahrentzen observes, "fundamental restructuring of the hidden program required sustained social, political, and historical insight and the ability to understand people and what they feel but can hardly say – skills generally not developed in architecture schools or while interning at architecture firms." See Sherry Ahrentzen, "The Space between the Studs: Feminism and Architecture," *Signs* 29, no. 1 (Autumn 2003): 192.

Moving through Grief

1. Postscript: Five years after Martin's death, Binnie bought a new house in a town which, like her childhood town, is in a walkable, close-knit community. She began to dance three times a week and, through dance, met a new partner who now has moved in with her.

CHAPTER 7
Conclusion

1. AIA, "Equity, Diversity and Inclusion Executive Summary."

2. Kroloff, "Gentleman's Profession."

3. Kroloff.

4. AIA, "Race and Equity at AIA," accessed December 14, 2021, aia.org/pages/6303978-race-and-equity-at-aia.

5. In *The Thinking Hand*, Juhani Pallasmaa suggests, "The main objective of artistic education may not directly reside in the principles of artistic making, but in the emancipation and opening up of the personality of the student and his/her self-awareness and self-image in relation to the immensely rich traditions of art, and to the lived world at large." Pallasmaa, *The Thinking Hand: Existential and Embodied Wisdom in Architecture* (Sussex: Wiley, 2009), 20.

6. Steinem, *Revolution*, 313.

Bibliography

Bibliography

Ahrentzen, Sherry. "The 'F' Word in Architecture: Feminist Analyses in/of/for Architecture." In *Reconstructing Architecture: Critical Discourses and Social Practices*, edited by Thomas A. Dutton and Lian Hurst Mann, 71–118. Minneapolis: University of Minnesota Press, 1996.

———. *"The Space between the Studs: Feminism and Architecture." Signs 29, no. 1 (2003): 179–206.*

AIA. "Equity, Diversity, and Inclusion Commission Report." January 5, 2017. https://content.aia.org/sites/default/files/2017-01/Diversity-EquityDiversityInclusionCommission-FINAL.pdf

———."Race and Equity at AIA." Accessed December 14, 2021. aia.org/pages/6303978-race-and-equity-at-aia.

Alexander, Christopher. *The Nature of Order: An Essay on the Art of Building and the*
———. *Nature of the Universe (Book One: The Phenomenon of Life).* Berkeley: The Center for Environmental Structure, 2002.

———. *The Nature of Order: An Essay on the Art of Building and the Nature of the Universe (Book Two: The Process of Creating Life)*. Berkeley: The Center for Environmental Structure, 2002.

———. *The Nature of Order: An Essay on the Art of Building and the Nature of the Universe (Book 4: Luminous Ground)*. Berkeley: The Center for Environmental Structure, 2002.

Anthony, Kathryn. *Designing for Diversity: Gender, Race, and Ethnicity in the Architectural Profession*. Champaign: University of Illinois Press, 2007.

Arieff, Allison. "Where Are All the Female Architects?" *The New York Times*, December 16, 2018.

Augustin, Sally. *Designology: How to Find Your PlaceType & Align Your Life with Design*. Coral Gables: Mango Publishing Group, 2019.

Bachelard, Gaston. *The Poetics of Space*. Boston: Beacon Press, 1964.

Baldwin, Eric. "World Trade Center Transportation Hub Oculus Designed in Remembrance of 9/11." *ArchDaily*, September 11, 2008. https://www.archdaily.com/901840/world-trade-center-transportation-hub-oculus-designed-in-remembrance-of-9-11.

Battarbee, Katja, Jane Fulton Suri, and Suzanne Gibbs Howard. "Empathy on the Edge: Scaling and Sustaining a Human-Centered Approach in the Evolving Practice of Design." IDEO. https://new-ideo-com.s3.amazonaws.com/assets/files/pdfs/news/Empathy_on_the_Edge.pdf

Battino, Rubin. *Metaphoria: Metaphor and Guided Metaphor for Psychotherapy and Healing*. Norwalk, CT: Crown House Publishing Ltd., 2005.

Bertrand, Wendy. *Enamored with Place: As Woman + As Architect*. San Francisco: Eye on Place Press, 2015.

Beth, Amy, "Libraries and the Missing Narrative: Practitioner Explorations in the use of Design Psychology and Environmental Autobiography for Library Buildings and Designs." CUNY Academic Works, 2018. https://academicworks.cuny.edu/gc_etds/2504

Billcliffe, Roger. *Charles Rennie Mackintosh and the Art of the Four*. London: Frances Lincoln, 2017.

Borneman, Elizabeth. "Study Suggests that Men Aren't Better at Reading Maps Than Women." October 1, 2016, accessed Dec. 13, 2021. https://www.geographyrealm.com/study-suggests-men-arent-better-reading-maps-women/.

Boutelle, Sarah Holmes. *Julia Morgan, Architect*. New York: Abbeville Press Publishers, 1995.

Breakfast Club. "How Gloria Steinem is Using Her Home to Create A Safe Space for Women." November 4, 2020. https://thebreakfastclub.iheart.com/featured/breakfast-club/content/2020-11-04-how-gloria-steinem-is-using-her-home-to-create-a-safe-space-for-women/ (accessed November 30, 2021).

Brett, David. *C. R. Mackintosh: The Poetics of Workmanship*. London: Reaktion Books, 1992.

Broude, Norma and Mary D. Garrard. *The Power of Feminist Art: The American Movement of the 1970s, History and Impact*. New York: Harry N. Abrams, Inc., 1994.

Brown, Denise Scott. *Having Words*. London: Architectural Association, 2009.

Burkhauser, Jude, ed. *Glasgow Girls: Women in Art and Design 1880–1920*. Edinburgh: Cannongate Publishing Limited, 1990.

Campbell, Joseph. *The Hero With a Thousand Faces*. New York: Bollingen Foundation, 1949.

———. *Pathways to Bliss: Mythology and Personal Transformation*. Novado, CA: New World Library, 2004.

Campbell, Joseph and Bill Moyers. *Joseph Campbell and the Power of Myth, with Bill Moyers*. St. Paul, MN: High Bridge, 1988. Audiotape.

Cigliano Hartman, Jan, Andraos, et.al., ed., *The Women Who Changed Architecture*. New York: Princeton Architectural Press, 2022.

Cobb, Edith. *The Ecology of the Imagination in Childhood*. New York: Columbia University Press, 1977.

Cohen, Laurie. *Imagining Women's Careers*. Oxford: Oxford University Press, 2014.

Coleman, Daniel. *Emotional Intelligence*. New York: Bantam, 1997.

Cooper Marcus, Clare. *House as Mirror of Self*. Berkeley: Conari Press, 1995.

———. "The House as a Symbol of Self." In *Environmental Psychology: People and Their Physical Settings*, edited by W. Ittelson, L. Rivlin and H. Proshansky, 435–448. New York: Holt, Rinehart and Winston, 1976.

———. *Iona Dreaming: The Healing Power of Place, A Memoir*. Lake Worth, FL: Nicolas Hays, Inc., 2010.

Cramer, Ned. "Men of Architecture." *Architect Magazine*, March 21, 2018. https://www.architectmagazine.com/design/editorial/men-of-architecture_0.

Csikszentmihalyi, Mihaly. *Flow: The Psychology of Optimal Experience*. New York: Harper Perennial, 1990.

de Mille, Richard. *Put Your Mother on the Ceiling*. New York: Penguin Books, 1976.

de Wolfe, Elsie. *The House of Good Taste*. 1913. Reprint, Las Vegas: Jefferson Publication, 2015.

Decq, Odile. "Being a Woman in the Architectural Field." In *Women in Architecture: From History to Future*, edited by Ursula Schwitalla. Berlin: Hatje Cantz, 2021.

Doyle, Michelle. "Eileen Gray: an architect and designer you should know." RA. March 20, 2020. Accessed November 29, 2021. https://www.royalacademy.org.uk/article/eileen-gray-architect-designer.

Drucker, Sally Ann. "Betty Friedan: The Three Waves of Feminism." OH Blog and News, April 27, 2018. https://www.scribd.com/document/409916898/Betty-Friedan-the-Three-Waves-of-Feminism-Ohio-Humanities.

Dutton, Thomas A. and Lian Hurst Mann. *Reconstructing Architecture Critical Discourses and Social Practices*. Minneapolis: University of Minnesota Press, 1996.

Farrow, Clare. *Childhood ReCollections: Memory and Design*. London: Roca, 2015. Exhibition catalog.

Fausch, Deborah. "She Said, He Said: Denise Scott Brown and Kenneth Frampton on Popular Taste." *FOOTPRINT* (Spring 2011): 77–90.

Favro, Diane. "Sincere and Good: The Architectural Practice of Julia Morgan." Special Issue, Women's Voices in Architecture and Planning, *Journal of Architectural and Planning Research* 9, no. 2 (Summer 1992): 112–128.

Field Belenky, Mary, Blythe McVicker Clinchy, Nancy Rule Goldberger, and Jill Mattuck Tarule. *Women's Ways of Knowing: The Development of Self, Voice, and Mind*. Basic Books, 1986.

Franck, Karen A. "A Feminist Approach to Architecture: Acknowledging Women's Ways of Knowing." In *Architecture: A Place for Women*, edited by Ellen Perry Berkeley and Matilda McQuaid, 201–216. Washington: The Smithsonian Institution Press, 1989.

Freire, Paulo. *Pedagogy of the Oppressed*. New York: Continuum, 1970.

Freud, Esther. *Mr. Mac and Me*. New York: Bloomsbury Publishing, 2014.

Friedan, Betty. *The Feminine Mystique*. New York: W.W. Norton & Company, 1963.

Fulton Suri, Jane. Interview by Nina Azzarello. DesignBoom. April 25, 2016. https://www.designboom.com/design/jane-fulton-suri-interview-ideo-little-book-of-design-research-ethics-04-25-2016/.

———. *Thoughtless Acts? Observations on Intuitive Design*. San Francisco: Chronicle Books, 2005.

Gamolina, Julia. "Julia Gamolina on Breaking the Architect's Mold." Interview by Alexandra Siebenthal. reSITE. November, 2020. https://www.resite.org/stories/julia-gamolina-on-breaking-the-architects-mold.

———. "Stop asking where all the female architects are; we're right here." *Madame Architect*. Accessed December 11, 2021. https://www.archpaper.com/2018/12/madame-architect-op-ed/?amp=1.

Gans, Herbert. *Popular Culture and High Culture: An Analysis and Evaluation of Taste*. New York: Basic Books, 1974.

Gappell, Millicent. "Psychoneuroimmunology." In *Innovations in Healthcare Design*, edited by Sara O. Marberry, 116. New York: Van Nostrand Reinhold, 1995.

Garcia, Hector, and Francesc Miralles. *Ikigai: The Japanese Secret to a Long and Happy Life*. New York: Penguin Random House LLC, 2016.

Gianoulis, Tina, and Claude J. Summers. "Interior Design." *GLBTQ*, 2015. http://www.glbtqarchive.com/arts/interior_design_A.pdf.

Gloria's Foundation. Accessed November 30, 2021. https://www.gloriasfoundation.org/.

———. "A Home for a Movement." Accessed November 30, 2021. https://artsandculture.google.com/story/a-home-for-a-movement/jgIi1197UxiDIA.

Goleman, Daniel. *Emotional Intelligence*. New York: Bantam Books, 1995.

Hadid, Zaha. "520W28." Accessed December 3, 2021. https://www.520w28.com/architecture.

Hall, Jane. *Breaking Ground: Architecture by Women*. Phaidon Press, 2019.

Havenhand, Lucinda Kaukas. "A Re-View from the Margin: Interior Design." *Design Issues* 35, no. 1 (Winter 2019): 67–72.

———. "A View from the Margin: Interior Design." *Design Issues* 20, No. 4 (Autumn 2004): 32–42.

Helland, Janice. "Frances Macdonald: The Self as Fin-de-Siecle Woman." *Woman's Art Journal* (Spring-Summer 1993): 15–22.

———. *The Studios of Frances and Margaret Macdonald*. Manchester: Manchester University Press, 1996.

Hewitt, Mark Alan. *Draw in Order to See: A Cognitive History of Architectural Design*. Oro Editions, 2020.

Hochman, Anndee. "Inner Realms." *The Philadelphia Enquirer*, January 5, 2007.

Hooks, Bell. *All About Love*. New York: William Morrow and Company, Inc., 2018.

Hudson, Kim. *The Virgin's Promise*. Studio City, CA: Michael Wiese Productions, 2010.

Huelat, Barbara J. *Healing Environments: Design for the Body, Mind & Spirit*. Alexandria, VA: Mede-zyn, 2003.

Iannacci, Anthony (ed.). *Developing the Architecture of the Workplace: Gensler 1967-1997*. New York: Edizioni Press, Inc., 1998.

Israel, Toby. "Metaphoria by Design." Design on My Mind (blog), *Psychology Today*, November 15, 2017. https://www.psychologytoday.com/us/node/1108748/preview.

———. "Women by Design: Transforming Home, Transforming Self, Part I: The Three Muses." Design on My Mind (blog), *Psychology Today*, July 2, 2015. https://www.psychologytoday.com/us/node/1076830/preview.

———. *Some Place Like Home: Using Design Psychology to Create Ideal Places*. Chichester: Wiley/Academy Editions, 2003.

———. The Art and the Environment Experience: Reactions to Public Murals in England. PhD diss., City University of New York, 1988.

Jameson, Marni. *Downsizing the Blended Home*. New York: Stirling, 2019.

Jencks, Charles, and Edwin Heathcote. *The Architecture of Hope*. London: Frances Lincoln, 2010.

Kandel, Eric R. *The Age of Insight: The Quest to Understand the Unconscious in Art, Mind, and Brain*. New York: Random House, 2012.

Kastner, Victoria. *Julia Morgan: An Intimate Biography of the Trailblazing Architect*. San Francisco: Chronicle Books, 2022.

Kaufman, Leslie. "William Moggridge, Designer and Laptop Pioneer, Dies at 69." *New York Times*, September 12, 2012.

Kaufman, Scott Barry. *Transcend: The New Science of Self-Actualization*. New York: TarcherPerigee, 2020.

Keirsey, David and Marilyn Bates. *Please Understand Me: Character, Temperament and Types*. Del Mar, CA.: Gnostic, 1984.

Kelly, Tom, and Johnathan Littman. *The Ten Faces of Innovation: IDEO's Strategies for Beating the Devil's Advocate and Driving Creativity Throughout Your Organization*. New York: Doubleday, 2005.

Keswick Jencks, Maggie. *A View from the Front Line*. London: Maggie Keswick and Charles Jencks, 1995.

Kinchin, Judith, Liz Bird, and Thomas Howarth. "Second City of the Empire.'" In *Glasgow Girls: Women in Art and Design 1880–1920*, edited by Jude Burkhauser, 27–42. (Edinburgh: Cannongate Publishing Limited, 1990).

Kirkham, Pat, ed. *Women Designers in the USA 1900-2000: Diversity and Difference*. New Haven: Yale University Press, 2000.

Kleinman, Kent, Joanna, Merwood-Salisbury, and Lois Weinthal. *After Taste: Expanded Practice in Interior Design*. New York: Princeton Architectural Press, 2012.

Kolko, Jon. *Thought on Interaction Design*. Savannah: Brown Bear, 2007.

Kroloff, Reed. "Architecture Is No Longer Just a 'Gentleman's Profession.'" *The New York Times*, September 14, 2018.

Lewis, Anna M. *Women of Stone and Steel*. Chicago: Chicago Review Press, 2014.

Linn, Will. "Joseph Campbell Is the Hidden Link Between '2001,' 'Star Wars,' and 'Mad Max: Fury Road.'" *IndieWire*, March 12, 2018. https://www.indiewire.com/2018/03/joseph-campbell-heros-journey-2001-star-wars-1201937470/.

Loden, Marilyn. *How to Succeed in Business Without Being One of the Boys*. New York: Times Books, 1985.

Lowden, Nancy, ed. *Doris Leeper: Legacy of a Visionary*. Cocoa, FL: Florida Historical Society Press, 2016.

Maslow, Abraham. *Motivation and Personality*. New York: Harper and Row, 1954.

Matthews, Carl and Caroline Hill. "Gay Until Proven Straight: Exploring Perceptions of Male Interior Designers from Male Practitioner and Student Perspectives." *Journal of Interior Design* 36 (2011): 15–34.

McCulloch, Gretchen. "We Learned to Write the Way We Talk." *The New York Times*, December 29, 2019.

McNeill, Karen. "Julia Morgan: Gender, Architecture, and Professional Style." *Pacific Historical Review* 76, No. 2 (May 2007): 229–268.

Moggridge, Bill. *Designing Interactions*. Cambridge, MA: MIT Press, 2007.

Murdock, Maureen. *The Heroine's Journey*. Boston: Shambhala Publications, Inc., 1990.

Murphy Paul, Annie. *The Extended Mind: The Power of Thinking Outside the Brain*. Boston: Houghton Mifflin Harcourt, 2021.

Naparstek, Bellaruth. *Invisible Heroes: Survivors of Trauma and How They Heal*. New York: Bantam Books, 2004.

———. *Staying Well with Guided Imagery*. New York: Wellness Central, 1994.

Napier, Nancy J. *Recreating Your Self: Building Self-Esteem Through Imaging and Self-Hypnosis*. New York: Norton, 1990.

Neat, Timothy. *Part Seen, Part Imagined: Meaning and Symbolism in the Work of Charles Rennie Mackintosh and Margaret Macdonald*. Edinburgh: Cannongate Press, 1994.

Ngozi Adichie, Chimamanda. *We Should All Be Feminists*. New York: Anchor Books, 2012.

O'Brien, Timothy A., with Margo Grant Walsh. *Collecting by Design: Silver & Metalwork of the Twentieth Century from the Margo Grant Walsh Collection*. Houston: The Museum of Fine Arts, Houston, 2008.

Osbon, Diane K., ed. *Reflections on the Art of Living: A Joseph Campbell Companion*. New York: Harper Collins Publishers, 1991.

Pable, Jill. "Interior Design Identity in the Crossfire: A Call for Renewed Balance in Subjective and Objective Ways of Knowing." *Journal of Interior Design* 34, no. 2 (January 2009): v–xx.

Pallasmaa, Juhani. *The Eyes of the Skin: Architecture and the Senses*. New York: John Wiley, 2005.

———. *The Thinking Hand*. Chichester: John Wiley, 2009.

Parker, Priya. *The Art of Gathering: How We Meet and Why it Matters*. New York: Riverhead Books, 2018.

Perkins, Sam. "Margo Grant Walsh 1936 – Present." *Silent Masters*, accessed September 28, 2021, https://silentmasters.net/article/margo-grant/.

Perry Berkeley, with Ellen Perry, ed., and Matilda McQuaid, assoc. ed. *Architecture: A Place for Women*. Washington and London: Smithsonian Institution Press, 1989.

Pile, John. *A History of Interior Design*. Hoboken: John Wiley & Sons, Inc., 2005.

Pinkola Estes, Clarissa. *Women Who Run With the Wolves: Myths and Stories of the Wild Woman Archetype*. River Wolf Press, 2017. Kindle.

Play and Playground Encyclopedia. "Betsy Caesar." Accessed December 14, 2021. https://www.pgpedia.com/c/betsy-caesar.

Preston, Jennifer. "Design With Consideration: Jennifer Preston on Listening Fully and Finding Her Power." Interview by Julia Gamolina, *Madame Architect*, April 12, 2018. https://www.madamearchitect.org/interviews/2018/4/24/design-with-consideration-jennifer-preston-on-listening-fully-and-finding-her-power.

Quacchi, Russell L. *Julia Morgan Architect and the Creation of the Asilomar Conference Gounds*. USA: Russell L. Quacchi, 2005.

QueerBio.com. "LGBTQ Interior Designers." February 21, 2020. https://queerbio.com/wiki/index.php/LGBTQ_Interior_Designers.

Rattner, Donald M. *My Creative Space: How to Design Your Home to Stimulate Ideas and Spark Innovation*. New York: Skyhorse Publishing, 2019.

Reiner, Andrew. *Better Boys, Better Men: The New Masculinity That Creates Greater Courage and Emotional Resiliency*. San Francisco: Harper One, 2020.

Rippon, Gina. *Gender and Our Brains: How New Neuroscience Explodes the Myth of the Female Brain*. New York: Pantheon Books, 2019.

Robert Venturi, Denise Scott Brown, and Steven Izenour. *Learning from Las Vegas*. Cambridge: MIT Press, 1972.

Rosen, Sidney, ed., Arens, Brian, et. al. *My Voice Will Go with You: The Teaching Tales of Milton H. Erikson*. New York: W. W. Norton & Company Ltd., 1991.

Rothchild, Joan, ed. *Design and Feminism: Re-Visioning Space, Places, and Everyday Things*. New Brunswick: Rutgers University Press, 1999.

Schachtel, Ernst. *Metamorphosis: On the Development of Affect, Perception, Attention, and Memory*. New York: Basic Books, 1959.

Schwitalla, Ursula, ed. *Women in Architecture: From History to Future*. Berlin: Hatje Cantz, 2021.

Scott Brown, Denise. *Having Words*. London: Architectural Association, 2009.

Sellers, Libby. *Women Design: Pioneers in Architecture, industrial, Graphic and Digital Design from the Twentieth Century to the Present Day*. London: Frances Lincoln, 2017.

Sparke, Penny. *An Introduction to Design and Culture.* London: Routledge, 2004.

———. *As Long As It's Pink: the Sexual Politics of Taste*. London: Pandora, 1995.

Steinem, Gloria. *My Life on the Road*. New York: Random House, 2015.

———. *Revolution from Within: A Book of Self-Esteem*. New York: Little, Brown and Company, 1992.

Sternberg, Esther. *Healing Spaces: The Science of Place and Well-being*. Cambridge: The Belknap Press, 2009.

———. *The Balance Within: The Science Connecting Health and Emotions*. New York: W. H. Freeman and Company, 2001.

Stone, Leilah. "In Defense of Decoration." *Metropolis*, Sept 22, 2020. https://www.metropolismag.com/interiors/residential-interiors/in-defense-of-decoration/.

Stratigakos, Despina. "Breaking the Cycle: Despina Stratigakos on Historical Amnesia, the Magic of Architecture, and Creating Conditions for Change." Interview by Julia Gamolina, *Madame Architect*, March 7, 2019. https://www.madamearchitect.org/interviews/2019/3/3/breaking-the-cycle-despina-stratigakos.

———. *Where Are the Women Architects?* Princeton: Princeton University Press, 2016.

Tartar, Maria. *The Heroine with 1,001 Faces.* New York: Liveright Publishing Corporation, 2021.

Tenenbaum, Jeremy Eric. *Downtown Denise Scott Brown*. Zurich: Architekturzentrum Wien and Park Books, 2018.

The Green School. "Student Wellbeing." Accessed November 30, 2021. https://www.greenschool.org/bali/student-wellbeing/.

Trubiano, Franca, Ramona Adlakha, and Ramune Bartuskaite, eds. *Women [Re]-Build: Stories Polemics Futures*. Novato CA, USA: Applied Research and Design/Oro Editions, 2019.

Turrell, Claire. "How a former DKNY designer launched an architecture firm in Bali that builds modern, million-dollar jungle mansions out of bamboo." *Insider.* June 14, 2021. Accessed October 21, 2021. https://www.insider.com/bamboo-mansions-bali-photos-elora-hardy-ibuku-feature-2021-6.

University of Oregon. "Margo Grant Walsh 1960: Remarkable career leads from Great Plains to global design work." Accessed September 22, 2021. http://design.uoregon.edu/margo-grant-walsh-1960.

Venturi, Robert. *Complexity and Contradiction in Architecture*. New York: Museum of Modern Art, 1977.

Venturi, Robert, Denise Scott Brown, and Steven Izenour. *Learning from Las Vegas*. Cambridge: MIT Press, 1972.

Wadsworth, Ginger. *Julia Morgan, Architect of Dreams*. Minneapolis: Lerner Publications Company, 1990.

Wakeman, Gregory. "Stay 'Home': new AppleTV+ show offers a glimpse at the world's most incredible abodes." *The National*. April 18, 2020. Accessed October 21, 2021. https://www.thenationalnews.com/arts-culture/television/stay-home-new-appletv-show-offers-a-glimpse-at-the-world-s-most-incredible-abodes-1.1007273.

White, Allison Carll. "What's in a Name? Interior Design and/or Interior Architecture: The Discussion Continues." *Journal of Interior Design* 35 (May 14, 2009): x–xviii.

Wikipedia. "Coverture." Accessed December 13, 2021. https://en.wikipedia.org/wiki/Coverture.

Wilson, Mark Anthony. *Julia Morgan: Architect of Beauty*. Layton, Utah: Gibbs Smith, Publisher, 2007.

Woolf, Virginia. *A Room of One's Own*. 1929. London: Hogarth Press, 1935.

Zaltman, Gerald. *How Customers Think: Essential Insights into the Mind of the Market*. Boston: Harvard Business School Press, 2003.

Zaltman, Gerald and Lindsay H. Zaltman. *Marketing Metaphoria: What Deep Metaphors Reveal about the Minds of Consumers*. Boston: Harvard Business Press, 2008.

Photograph by Tamara Gillon.

Toby Israel, Ph.D.

Toby Israel, Ph.D. is the founder of Design Psychology, a field that's gained international attention in the *L.A.*, *N.Y. and Financial Times*, *CBS Sunday Morning*, and NPR's "Talk of the Nation." Trained as an Environmental Psychologist, she is a multi-disciplinary design, psychology, arts and education professional who applies scholarship to the "real world" practice of place-making. For further information see www.designpsychology.net.